THE CROSS
IS THE KEY

Published by Legacy Press
Your life tells a story; we can help you write it.
LegacyPress.org

Terry@jterrymoore.org
4041 Marsh Lane
Carrollton, TX 75007

Unless otherwise noted, all Scripture references are taken from the NEW KING JAMES VERSION.
Copyright © 1979, 1980, 1982 by Thomas Nelson, Inc.

Cover and interior images are the property of their respective copyright holders from Shutterstock.

ISBN (print): 978-1-957026-00-8
ISBN (ebook): 978-1-957026-01-5

Cover Design by Michal Eldridge
Interior design and layout by Nelly Murariu @PixBeeDesign.com

ADVANCED FOUNDATIONS

The Cross Is the Key

The Purpose, Power, and the Victory of the Cross

TERRY MOORE

CONTENTS

Acknowledgments   vii

An Invitation to a New Way of Living   ix

Introduction   xiii

PART 1 – What Jesus Did for Us at the Cross   1

  1: What Really Happened at the Cross?   5

  2: The Purpose of the Cross   13

PART 2 – The Cross Represents the Love of God   23

  3: The Love of the Father   27

  4: How Do We Experience God's Love?   35

  5: Maturing in Christ   47

PART 3 – The Exchange of the Cross   65

  6: Our Inheritance as Heirs of God   69

  7: The Great Exchange   77

  8: The Essence of Faith   97

PART 4 – The Cross Defeated the Enemy   107

  9: After the Cross, the Resurrection   111

  10: The Complete Victory of the Cross   125

  11: The Power of Identification with Christ   143

PART 5 – Experiencing the Victorious Life   155

    12: Living in the Power of the Cross   159

    13: The Resurrected Life   173

    14: The Cross and Communion   187

A Word from the Author   191

In Closing …   194

Appendix   195

About the Author   218

More Titles Available in the Advanced Foundations Series   220

ACKNOWLEDGMENTS

I have so many people to thank for their input into my life that it would be impossible to mention all of them. However, I do want to thank those who have been directly responsible for this book.

First, I thank God for using James Robison to introduce Susan and me to the freedom and victory we now experience. We will be forever grateful for his boldness to proclaim the power of God, the truth of the Word, and the filling of the Holy Spirit in a way that cost him dearly.

I am thankful to Dudley Hall. His support and influence over the years have shaped and directed our lives into the grace of God and the truth that makes us free and keeps us free.

Obviously, this book and the life that I enjoy would not have been possible without a wonderful family. My wife, Susan, who has been a constant source of love and encouragement, along with our children David and Meredith, who are gifts from God and have been the strength of my life. We have also been blessed with a wonderful daughter-in-law, Christina, and with their two children, Elizabeth and Ethan and our son-in-law, Tate, and their three children, Catherine, Brooklyn, and Lauren.

I would be remiss not to thank my mother and father who gave me a wonderful Christian heritage and a godly home. I am grateful to my brother Bob and sister-in-law Kaye for their financial support, which has made this book possible.

I also want to thank those who have contributed to various parts of this book. Beth Clark, who worked on my first manual that has resulted in this book. Sunny Lerch, who helped turn my notes and messages into something that could be read and understood. Leslyn

Musch, who helped edit the manuscript. This 2nd edition is credited to Linda Hudson and Diana Perez, who spent numerous hours making tremendous revisions to clarify the message.

Lastly, I want to thank Ronna Keller, my executive assistant, who has worked long and hard to make sure that everything got done so this book could come into reality.

Thank you all for your part in this book. I pray that God will richly bless you and that God will use this book to help people experience the power of the Cross in their lives.

AN INVITATION TO
A NEW WAY OF LIVING

I believe that understanding the power of the Cross is vital for every believer. I can say with certainty that it has revolutionized my life and the life of the church I pastor. Anyone who has ever been frustrated, hurt, disappointed or simply looking for "more" in life can find the answers and hope in discovering what Jesus really did for us on the Cross.

Understanding the power of the Cross has been the key to everything I have ever needed in my spiritual walk and in my life. I was raised in a wonderful Christian home and have always attended church. I accepted Jesus as my personal Savior at an early age and tried to live my life as a "good Christian." I continued to attend church after I married my childhood sweetheart, Susan; I read my Bible and prayed on a regular basis, but I found I was not experiencing a victorious life. I knew Jesus died for me and saved me, but I don't remember ever hearing about what really happened on the Cross or being made aware of the awesome, life-changing blessings available to me through it.

By the time I was thirty-one years old, I found myself still going to church and reading my Bible on a daily basis but struggling with all kinds of issues that I knew were not godly. I could not understand what was wrong. I had a terrible temper, which I could not control. Emotionally, I would explode when I became angry. Physically, I broke things or tore apart whatever was around me. Verbally, I burst into tirades of profanity. These things happened frequently. Obviously, I knew these behaviors and outbursts weren't characteristic of a Christian, but I was powerless to gain control over this. I thank God that my anger never turned toward people; because I was so out of control, I could have hurt someone. After what I experienced, I can understand how people can violently hurt others in fits of rage.

In addition to my fierce temper, I could not control my thought life, meaning that I could not discipline myself mentally and was unable to focus for very long. Many mornings, I read my Bible, but by the afternoons I could not remember what I read. Besides the mental and spiritual condition I was in, I had taken what I thought was a considerable amount of money and turned it into a large amount of debt. Then, to make matters worse, I injured my back and was in tremendous pain. My struggles may not sound severe in comparison to the tragedies and suffering many people endure, but it was extremely frustrating, and it made my life very difficult. As someone who was a Christian, who attended church on a regular basis, who was surrounded by Christian friends and who had a godly wife and wonderful children, this set of circumstances made me desperate for something to change. I was in the prime of my life, in physical pain, with a temper that I could not control. And I sat in church each week feeling miserable, acting like there was no problem.

Since those days when I suffered silently, I have discovered there are many people in the same condition I was in. Churches are filled with people who have the same struggles or similar challenges that are just as intense, debilitating, or dangerous. These people attend church; they smile and say they are fine, when in reality they are angry, frustrated, hurting, or captive to negative emotions and circumstances—just like I was. Maybe you are one of them.

I know there is hope for everyone who is longing for life to be different and better. I know that complete transformation is possible, because it happened to me. In the summer of 1982, I had successful back surgery and later that summer attended James Robison's weekend retreat. At the retreat, God had mercy on me and changed my life forever. I was filled with the Holy Spirit and completely set free from anger. I received a deep, personal revelation of the love of the Father, and the Word of God came alive to me like never before. Literally overnight, I realized I had the ability to focus more clearly on Scripture. The Word of God came alive to me, and it was like I had complete clarity. It took me some time, a number of years, to get my financial position corrected, but that eventually happened too. That experience changed my life and set me on a course that continues today. I am pursuing God with all of my heart and have a desire to help others experience the same freedom I experienced.

One of the life-changing truths that led me into freedom and victory is that the key to a life of power, passion, peace, and joy is the Cross of Jesus Christ. It's not just a simple wooden structure or form, it's a vehicle and means of complete transformation for everyone who embraces its power. The Cross certainly represents Jesus's death for our sins, but it means much, much more.

I invite you to join me in discovering the various ways in which the Cross is the key to a revolution of love, freedom, and victory in your life.

Terry Moore

Founding Pastor and Elder, Sojourn Church, Carrolton, TX
Founder and President, International Apostolic Network, dba JTerryMoore.org

INTRODUCTION

God is amazing in the way He can use anything in our lives to teach us His ways, even a forgotten memory. As a young boy visiting my grandmother, I liked playing with an old skeleton key that hung in an antique armoire in her house. I liked to take the key out of the lock and play with it. My grandmother told me repeatedly not to lose it. So, of course, my goal was to hide it to see if I could get a rise out of my grandmother. I usually did.

Years later, long after I'd forgotten about playing with that old key during my childhood days, I was reading and meditating on Matthew 16, in which Jesus tells us that He would build His Church and give us the keys to the Kingdom. As I read, I saw in my mind's eye that old key. I knew the Lord was trying to show me something about His Kingdom, but I could not fully understand what He was saying.

Sometime after having that vision of the old key, I was watching Christian television and saw a minister preaching behind a clear plastic pulpit. I could hardly believe my eyes when I saw a very ornate Cross etched into the pulpit. The design of the Cross instantly reminded me of the old skeleton key from my grandmother's house. The Lord spoke to me, "The Cross is the Key—the key to everything." I began to understand that the Cross is the key to knowing God, to advancing His Kingdom, to loving one another, to health and wholeness, and to a full and victorious life. This understanding of the message of the Cross has directed my life and the life of Sojourn Church for years now. I believe it's vitally important for all of us.

That evening, the Holy Spirit began to give me divine revelation about the Cross and about the awesome power of what Jesus accomplished there through everything involved in His death, His burial,

and His resurrection. When I use the term, "the Cross," I am referring to *all* that Jesus did for us. In fact, the Cross represents one of
the greatest events in human history. What Jesus fulfilled on the
Cross and through the Cross sealed our victory forever! It looked
like defeat, but in reality, it was *the greatest victory of all time!*

Not only does the Cross represent the greatest *victory* of all time, it
is also the message of *hope* for all people. In this world there is pain,
hurt, sickness, evil and overall failure and futility. No one escapes
the pain and frustration that comes from being in a world permeated
by sin. But, when Jesus was raised from the dead to live forevermore,
He defeated death and gave life—eternal life—to all those who would
receive the message of the Cross.

Paul writes in 1 Corinthians 1:18: "For the message of the cross is
foolishness to those who are perishing, but to us who are being saved
it is the power of God." In other words, the message or word of the
Cross is actually silly to people who are perishing, but to those who
are being saved it is the power of God. If this is true, and I believe
it is, then we desperately need to understand and appropriate the
fullness of this message.

Let's think about why Paul might say the message seems foolish to
those who are perishing. If you were looking for a Savior, or a King,
or a Deliverer would you want one who was taken without a fight,
was crucified and died? Naturally, we want a hero, a victorious King,
in whom we can boast. Someone we view as the strong "leader type"
is the one we want as our King, one who boldly defeats enemies and
triumphs over all.

This brave profile certainly did not appear to describe Jesus. He
was meek and kind; yet He was strong—but not in a way that man
would expect. He had a small group of followers, never commanded
an army, and did not exert Himself on anyone. In fact, when the
crowds followed Him, He told them stories, which most of them did

not fully understand. He didn't appear to be the courageous, triumphant king people might have expected. But He was. That seems foolish to people who don't understand it. His death may even seem to be just another case of capital punishment. But it is powerful beyond description to those who know Jesus's love and grace.

This —the message of the power of the Cross—is where there is hope. Regardless of what you have done, or what has been done to you, there is hope. This hope is in the truth of the Cross: *Life* comes out of *death*. This does not make sense to our minds. But Jesus is not dead (even though He died); He is risen and lives forever more. He is not still hanging on a Cross. He is not in a grave. He is risen from the dead to live forevermore *ruling* and *reigning* at the right hand of the Father. Because He lives, we can live too. Because He overcame sin, the devil, the world and all that is within it, we can have life and victory also. Moreover, we can be used to help others experience the same!

Jesus brings life out of death and beauty out of ashes. You may have experienced death and defeat in your life. You may be experiencing it now, but you can have life and victory because of the Cross and the fact that Jesus is alive and the same yesterday, today and forever. You may think that your life is burned up, just ashes, but Jesus brings beauty out of ashes. You no longer have to be a victim. Because of the Cross, you can be a victor! If you want this life, *His power and victory in your life*, continue with me as we discover the message and power of the Cross.

I pray this book will open your eyes to the awesome victory of Jesus and all that He paid for us. I pray that God will give you the ability to understand the Cross and to live in its power as the reality of everything Jesus has done for you unfolds for you and changes your life completely. He suffered a horrible death so we could have life, not just a ticket to heaven. We are to experience life in Christ here and now and live in His victory. For Christians, the Cross is the key to unlocking the wonderful life we have in Jesus, because the message of the Cross is the power of God. I pray that the Cross and all that it means will become the power of God in your life. The Cross *is* the Key!

PART 1

What Jesus Did for Us at the Cross

"This was the Son of God,
who died an agonizing death
just for you, and just for me."

What Really Happened at the Cross?

When I write that "the Cross is the key," I am referring to the Cross in terms of everything that happened as Jesus hung on the Cross and after His death and resurrection approximately 2000 years ago. You and I live in a day when crucifixion is so far removed from us, we hardly have any idea how terrible this form of death was. Without a doubt, this ancient practice was one of the most gruesome and painful forms of death ever known to man.

Crucifixion was a form of capital punishment that the Romans perfected, and it had been used for many years prior to Jesus's death. When we read that Jesus went to the Cross for us, we usually do not realize the pain and suffering He experienced. The film *The Passion of The Christ* provides some insight into the brutality of crucifixion, but the truth is it was probably worse than that film depicted.

Each of the four New Testament Gospels includes an account of Jesus's crucifixion, but what specifically did Jesus have to experience?

First, Jesus appeared before the high priest, who examined Him. According to Matthew 26:67, "they spat in His face and beat Him and others struck Him with the palms of their hands." People probably struck Him with rods also, and this was just the beginning of the process. What a humiliating, painful experience!

Jesus was then taken before Pontius Pilate, the Roman governor. Even though Pilate found no fault in Jesus, he turned Him over to the soldiers because the Jews cried and screamed out for Him to be crucified. The crucifixion itself began with a violent whipping with a scourge, a whip made of leather straps and pieces of bone or metal tied in the end of the straps. This beating was so horrible that many died during it. Prior to the scourging, soldiers stripped the clothes from the person being punished, then stretched him out so his back was totally bare. They then began to beat the person across the back. They hit so hard that their blows cut through a person's skin, all the way to the bone. At that time, a scourging of forty lashes was a common punishment for a crime. Many times, forty lashes led to death. Jews routinely struck a person only thirty-nine times so they would not be accused of being responsible for someone's death. This type of scourging was a beating nearly unto death.

The biblical account in Matthew 27 says that they put a scarlet robe on Him and placed a twisted crown of thorns on His head. Jesus's back was cut through to the bone, bleeding and bruised and they put a robe on Him. How excruciating! Matthew 27:30, informs us "that they spat on Him and struck Him in the head with a reed." So not only was He near death as a result of the scourging, they continued to mock Him and beat Him on the head after they had put the crown of piercing thorns on His head. This alone would have caused tremendous pain and by this time blood was surely flowing from His back and from His head. All of this happened before He was nailed to the Cross. It was an awful form of punishment.

After being beaten, Jesus was expected to carry the crossbeam of the Cross to the place where they would crucify Him. The Scriptures tell us He was so weak by this time He could not bear the weight of the beam. The soldiers found a man named Simon of Cyrene and forced him to carry the crossbeam for Jesus.

When they arrived at the place of crucifixion, they pulled off His robe again. This would have caused additional pain and re-opened

His wounds, as the robe was probably covered in dried blood and stuck to His back.

Then they tied the crossbeam to the vertical shaft of the Cross. After securing the vertical and horizontal beams properly, they pounded large nails through Jesus's hands and feet, nailing them to the Cross. The actual places through which they drove the nails were selected to cause the most pain. In the hands, this place was probably through the wrists, where the hands and wrists connect. Driving nails through this particular location on the body would accomplish two things. First, the hands of the one crucified would not tear through, which could happen if nails went through the middle of the hands. Second, nails in this wrist area would sever the nerve that runs through it. Jesus was already beaten nearly to death and now this. This trauma alone, which was horrible, would have killed most people.

"They did not nail Jesus tightly to the Cross but left just enough slack so His body would literally hang there—another proven way to inflict the greatest possible amount of pain."

With Jesus's body nailed in place in such a way to guarantee maximum agony, they raised the Cross and then dropped it into its place in the ground with a jolt that certainly sent another wave of shock and pain through Jesus's body. They did not nail Jesus tightly to the Cross but left just enough slack so His body would literally hang there—another proven way to inflict the greatest possible amount of pain. Clearly, the Romans had perfected crucifixion as the worst form of death imaginable.

Experts who have studied this form of death report that the people being crucified had trouble breathing and would try to push themselves up so they could inhale or exhale. They strained to raise themselves up from the nails in their feet and nails in the hands, pushing against the rugged wood of the Cross, rubbing it against their backs, which were already open to the bone from their scourgings. I cannot imagine how painful this must have been.

After Jesus had been hanging on the Cross for some time, the soldiers pierced His side with a spear and Scripture tells us that blood and water came out. This would have caused even more pain.

An Act of Love

The reason we need to know about the gory details of the crucifixion is that Jesus went through such unthinkable agony for you and me. The crucifixion is not a myth, a fable or some kind of ancient story; Jesus really went to the Cross and experienced all this pain for us. Isaiah 53:10 says that it actually *pleased* the Lord to crush Christ and make His soul an offering for sin. What love the Father has for us.

Christ's crucifixion happened on a Friday. This particular day was both the start of the Sabbath (at sundown) and the annual Passover celebration. Since Jesus, a Jew, was crucified on a Friday, according to Jewish custom He would need to die before the beginning of the Sabbath, which took place at 6:00 pm on Friday. Because crucifixion was an extremely slow form of death for most people, the Roman soldiers would often break the legs of the people being crucified so they could no longer push/hold themselves up to breathe. This final trauma often killed them. Jesus's legs were not broken (Psalms 34:19-20 and John 19:33-36).

Jesus had already told His disciples that no one could take His life, but that He would lay it down willingly for us. At 3:00 pm, the same time as the Passover lamb was being slain for the atonement of the people of Israel, Jesus, the true Lamb of God, gave up His spirit saying, "Father, into Your hands I commit My spirit" (Luke 23:46). At the very moment Christ gave up His spirit, the veil in the temple was torn in two from top to bottom, indicating that the way into God's presence was now open to all who would believe in Jesus. Man could have never accomplished this; it was God who made the way for us. What an amazing God, and what amazing love He has for us.

Matthew 27:50-54 offers a powerful account of what happened the moment Jesus died:

> *And Jesus cried out again with a loud voice, and yielded up His spirit. Then, behold, the veil of the temple was torn in two from top to bottom; and the earth quaked, and the rocks were split, and the graves were opened; and many bodies of the saints who had fallen asleep were raised; and coming out of the graves after His resurrection, they went into the holy city and appeared to many. So when the centurion and those with him, who were guarding Jesus, saw the earthquake and the things that had happened, they feared greatly, saying, "Truly this was the Son of God!"*

Yes, this was the Son of God, who died an agonizing death *just for you*, and just for me.

SUMMARY

† Christ was spat upon, hit and humiliated after being examined by the High Priest.

† Pontius Pilate found no fault in Jesus but turned Him over to the soldiers anyway to appease the cries of the Jewish people.

† Jesus was dressed in a scarlet robe and had a crown of thorns placed upon His head in an act of mockery because He had been called the King of the Jews.

† Jesus's hands and feet were nailed to the Cross.

† Jesus was pierced in the side with a spear—blood and water came out.

† Christ told His disciples that no one could take His life, so He yielded His spirit to God. At that very moment, the veil of the temple was torn in two from top to bottom, indicating that the way into God's presence was now open to all who would believe in Jesus Christ.

† God Himself made a way for us to be in intimate relationship with Him. As human beings, we could never do this for ourselves or for others.

The Purpose of the Cross

When we become aware of the hideous realities of death by crucifixion and begin to understand the agonizing sacrifice Jesus made for us, we have to ask, "Why? Why would He willingly suffer so intensely? Why would He choose to give up His life in such a painful way for us?"

To comprehend why the Cross was necessary, we need to start by looking at the very beginning of human life on earth. Genesis 1:27 tells us that God created mankind in His image and likeness. He designed and made us to be in fellowship with Him. His desire was to have a relationship with His creation and to fellowship with each of us.

Unfortunately for all of us, the first man God created, Adam, rebelled against God, thus committing sin. When Adam and Eve sinned in the Garden of Eden, they rejected the pure and intimate fellowship for which God created them and which they had once enjoyed with Him. Romans 5:12 tell us "Therefore, just as through one man [Adam] sin entered the world, and death through sin, and thus death spread to all men, because all sinned." Adam and Eve's sin not only built a barrier between God and them, but between God and everyone who would live on earth after them. That first sin in the Garden brought sin upon the entire human race.

Sin is not simply doing terrible things; to sin is to live our lives the way we choose or not giving God His rightful place in our lives. In Isaiah 53:6, we see that each of us "like sheep" have gone astray; every one of us has turned to our own way.

The sin into which we are born separates us from God and hinders intimate relationship with Him. Romans 3:23 says, "all have sinned and fall short of the glory of God," and Romans 6:23 says, "the wages of sin is death…" The problem of sin is what God determined to solve, ultimately, at the Cross.

God's Old Testament Sin Solution

Sin is costly. Sin separated Adam and Eve from God and continues to separate people from God today. Because He wanted a restored relationship with Adam and Eve, God had to make a sacrifice to cover their sin. After they sinned in the Garden, God had to kill an innocent animal to make coverings for them because their sin caused them to realize they were naked, and they were ashamed.

From the beginning of human history, blood has been required to cover sin. In Leviticus 17:11, God says, "For the life of the flesh is in the blood, and I have given it to you upon the altar to make atonement for your souls; for it is the blood that makes atonement for the soul." In fact, when the writer of the New Testament Book of Hebrews looked back to the Old Testament sacrifices to explain the parallels between the Old Testament system and Jesus's sacrifice on the Cross, he reminded us that "without the shedding of blood there is no remission" (Hebrews 9:22).

"Sin always demands death and causes death (see Romans 6:23)."

Sin always demands death and causes death (see Romans 6:23). In the Old Testament, during the time just prior to the Israelites' exodus from Egypt, the Lord brought several plagues on the land and people of Egypt because the Egyptian Pharaoh was continuing to hold God's people captive against God's will. In Exodus chapters 7-10, the

Lord sent Moses to tell Pharaoh to release His people; each time Pharaoh refused, the Lord sent another plague.

For the tenth and final plague, the Lord declared that, "all the first-born in the land of Egypt shall die" (Exodus 11:5). In order to spare His people, Israel, from experiencing death in their families, He commanded the Israelite families to sacrifice a lamb without blemish (see Exodus 12:5). Upon the sacrifice of the lamb, the Israelites were instructed to mark the doorpost of their homes with the blood from the spotless lamb. During the night, the death angel would pass by the homes in Egypt. If there was blood on the doorpost, the death angel would pass over that home and the firstborn son would not die. As the Lord said in Exodus 12:13, "Now the blood shall be a sign for you on the houses where you are. And when I see the blood, I will pass over you; and the plague shall not be on you to destroy you when I strike the land of Egypt."

After the children of Israel came out from under the Egyptian oppression and began their journey through the wilderness, the Lord spoke to Moses saying, "Speak to the children of Israel … And let them make Me a sanctuary, that I may dwell among them" (Exodus 25:2, 8). This sanctuary was called the tabernacle in the wilderness and referred to the tabernacle of Moses. The whole purpose of this tabernacle was to facilitate relationship between the holy God and His children.

God was making a way to cover the people and protect them from the coming judgment. He redeemed His people so they could be reconciled to Him and enjoy the intimate relationship with Him that was lost through sin in the Garden.

Why did the Lord want to be near them? Because He loved them so much. God has always desired to be with His people; He wants very much for us to receive His love. Again, God desires to do more than "save" us, He wants to have a relationship with us. He wants to fellowship with you! He wants to relate to you! He wants more than to call you His child; He wants to know you and He wants you to know Him too. The only way for that to happen is through relationship.

Exodus describes the tabernacle as being divided into sections. People could come inside the tabernacle into the Outer Court. A smaller area inside the tabernacle was designated as the Holy Place. God's presence rested even further into the Holy Place in the Most Holy Place with the Ark of the Covenant, a piece of furniture like a chest made from acacia wood and covered with gold. The Ark of the Covenant had the atonement cover or mercy seat resting atop it. Inside the Ark were three objects: manna, which God provided for the Israelites during their journey through the wilderness; Aaron's budded rod, which represented God's choosing of Aaron for the priesthood; and the stone tablets containing the Ten Commandments.

Some Bible translations call this Most Holy Place that housed God's presence the "Holy of Holies." The High Priest could only enter the Holy of Holies once per year; no one else was allowed to enter. The High Priest was human, therefore a sinner by nature, and only after an elaborate process of purification and blood sacrifice could he enter the Most Holy Place. Do you see the pattern here? Throughout the Old Testament, sin could only be atoned for by blood sacrifice.

The problem with this Old Testament practice was that it only covered and atoned for sin on an annual basis. Each year on the Day of Atonement, the High Priest would go before God and sprinkle the blood of a spotless lamb on the mercy seat of the Ark of the Covenant. That would cover or atone for the sins of the people for that year (see Leviticus 16 for a thorough explanation of the process of atonement).

God's New Testament Sin Solution

> For Christ has not entered the holy places made with hands,
> which are copies of the true, but into Heaven itself, now to
> appear in the presence of God for us; not that He should
> offer Himself often, as the high priest enters the Most Holy
> Place every year with blood of another—He then would
> have had to suffer often since the foundation of the world;
> but now, once at the end of the ages, He has appeared to put
> away sin by the sacrifice of Himself.
>
> Hebrews 9:24-26

In the New Testament, Jesus came to Earth as the Lamb of God,
the final sacrifice who would forever satisfy the need to atone for
sin. Everything the sacrificial lambs accomplished in the Old
Testament's yearly process of atonement; Jesus accomplished in the
New Testament with a single act of sacrifice. His one sacrifice on the
Cross paid for all sin for all time.

For a greater understanding of Jesus's complete payment for sin, I
encourage you to read all of Hebrews 9 and 10. These chapters make
clear that Jesus was not only the sacrifice for sin, but He was also
our High Priest, who offered Himself to the Father to pay for all of
our sin.

Remember, sin requires death. Jesus's death delivers us from sin and
redeems us forever. The blood of animals could never pay for sin. It
could only temporarily atone, one year at a time. But Jesus made the
final, lasting sacrifice. He is the only solution to the conflict between
holiness and sin. Now the payment for sin is complete.

The work of the Cross is a finished work—forever. The New Testament
Scriptures below affirm Jesus as the eternal Lamb of God, who has
paid in full the price for our sin.

The Apostle John writes about Jesus in John 1:29: "Behold, the Lamb of God who takes away the sin of the world!" and in Revelation 5:6: "And I looked, and behold, in the midst of the throne and of the four living creatures, and in the midst of the elders, stood a Lamb as though it had been slain …"

Not only did Jesus die for our sin, He actually *became* sin so we could be made righteous. Jesus Christ Himself was free of sin, but He took our sins upon Himself. God loved us so much that He not only gave His only Son to pay for our sin, but Jesus became sin. This pleased the Father because it was the only way for us to enter into relationship with Him. God saw us dead in sin. He knew that we were "dead in our trespasses," but He wanted a relationship with us so much that He allowed Jesus to take all sin upon Himself and pay its penalty once and for all.

The verses below help explain what God did for us, through Jesus, out of His awesome love:

> For He made Him who knew no sin to be sin for us, that we might become the righteousness of God in Him.
>
> 2 Corinthians 5:21

> For when we were still without strength, in due time Christ died for the ungodly.
>
> Romans 5:6

God loved each one of us so much, that He made provision for us before we knew we needed it, before we even asked for it. His desire for relationship with us outweighed His need for justice. Just like in the Old Testament where He redeemed His people, Israel, so they could be reconciled to Him, God has done the same and better for us. His love for us overcame sin. Now we can enjoy the relationship, intimacy, and fellowship with our loving Father that we could not have any other way.

> But God demonstrates His own love toward us, in that while we were still sinners, Christ died for us. Much more then, having now been justified by His blood, we shall be saved from wrath through Him.
>
> Romans 5:8- 9

> And you, being dead in your trespasses and the uncircumcision of your flesh, He has made alive together with Him, having forgiven you all trespasses, having wiped out the handwriting of requirements that was against us, which was contrary to us. And He has taken it out of the way, having nailed it to the cross.
>
> Colossians 2:13- 14

> He who believes in the Son has everlasting life; and he who does not believe the Son shall not see life, but the wrath of God abides on him.
>
> John 3:36

We are either joined to God and we have life, or we are separated from Him and we have death and the wrath of God is upon us. There is no in-between position. We need to turn from death and receive life; and we can do this only through the power of the Cross. The love of the Father, expressed through the Cross, gives us life—joyful, peaceful, powerful life now and life forever with Him.

God's desire is to give us life—not just a ticket to Heaven, but a glorious intimate relationship with Him, a relationship that begins on earth and is made possible through the Cross.

"God's desire is to give us life— not just a ticket to Heaven."

SUMMARY

† We were born in sin through Adam's sin.

† Sin is costly.

† Sin separates us from God.

† Sin requires death.

† The Old Testament solution—the blood sacrifice of an animal—atoned for sin on a yearly basis. This was a temporary solution.

† The New Testament solution—Jesus—atoned for sin once, for all time. This was an eternal solution.

† The work of the Cross is a complete work forever.

† God made provision for us before we knew we needed it.

† God's desire is to give us life—an intimate relationship with Him.

† Jesus became sin so we could be made righteous.

† We have to accept the sacrifice that Christ made for us, repent and turn from our former ways (death), and choose to walk with Him, completely forgiven of our sins (life).

♥ TAKE IT TO HEART

What does the Cross represent to you personally? As you have read through these chapters and prayed, God through His Holy Spirit has no doubt impressed upon you some things about your own life and the choices you have made. Perhaps concerning sin, your own righteousness or assurance about forgiveness and eternal life? Have you made that decision to accept Jesus's sacrifice on the Cross for your sins? And perhaps you need the Father's love in a very real way being demonstrated or made manifest to you? Ask Him to forgive you of your sin and then receive complete forgiveness and eternal life that only comes through Jesus Christ, the spotless Lamb of God.

𓂀 TAKE IT TO GOD

Dear Father God,

I come humbly before You and thank You for the finished work of Christ on the Cross that made an exchange for me. I'm grateful for His sacrifice that paid my debt and the penalty for my sins, that purchased my freedom, cleanses me from unrighteousness and grants me eternal life. I receive this gift of love and the amazing chance for an intimate, wonderful relationship with You. May I never forget the depths of that LOVE.

In Jesus's name. Amen.

Part 2

The Cross Represents the Love of God

"Truly, the Cross represents God's awesome love for us."

The Love of the Father

The most basic, but most profound truth of the Cross is that it represents the awesome, incredible, perfect love of our heavenly Father for us. We have already begun to understand the reason for the Cross and examined the horrible death that Jesus suffered for us. All of this should cause us to be overwhelmed with how much He loves us.

I believe the most important thing we need is a revelation of the Father's love for us. God wants us to know His love, which will change and transform every aspect of our lives. He not only wants us to know with our minds that He loves us; He is longing for us to have a deep and powerful revelation of His love in our hearts.

If you have ever attended church, you have probably heard John 3:16, "For God so loved the world that He gave His only begotten Son, that whoever believes in Him should not perish but have everlasting life." This verse is one of the most popular and most frequently quoted Scriptures in the Bible. But the question is: Who do you think of when you read, "God so loved the world"? Do you immediately identify yourself with "the world" and take this Scripture personally? Or do you think of "the world" as millions of people in lots of different countries all over the earth, without really counting yourself among them?

Many people never personalize John 3:16; they never really believe that the God of creation loves us so much that He would give His Son, His most treasured possession, to live and die for us. But we must understand that we are included when this verse says, "God so loved the world ... "

The first key to appropriating the power and provision of the Cross is to be established in the Father's intimate, personal, overwhelming love for you. He loves you so much that He sent His only Son to die for you. He loves you personally and wonderfully, just the way you are. We need to know His love not only in our minds, but deep in our hearts.

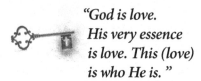

"God is love. His very essence is love. This (love) is who He is."

First John 4:8, teaches us that God is love. His very essence is love. This (love) is who He is. What an awesome God we have, that He would love us so much that He would give us His Son, Jesus and that Jesus would voluntarily go to the Cross for you and me.

The Apostle John wrote often about the love of God. In 1 John 4:9-10, he says: "In this the love of God was manifested toward us, that God has sent His only begotten Son into the world, that we might live through Him. In this is love, not that we loved God, but that He loved us and sent His Son to be the propitiation for our sins."

Notice the word *propitiation*. Most of us are not familiar with this word, but it's one we need to understand. In the *Spirit-Filled Life Bible,* the Word Wealth sidebar at 1 John 4:10 defines *propitiation* as the word that "describes Christ, through His sacrificial death, as appeasing the wrath of God on account of sin." His death serves as "a covering for sin. By means of the atoning death of Christ, God can be merciful to the sinner who believes in Him, and reconciliation is affected."

Many of us believe that God is angry with us. This is not true. *God is love;* sin provokes His wrath, but He placed that wrath on Jesus at the Cross so we could experience His love. Romans 5:9 underscores this point: "Much more then, having now been justified by His blood, we shall be saved from wrath through Him."

First Thessalonians 5:9 also affirms the fact that Jesus took God's wrath on our behalf: "For God did not appoint us to wrath, but to obtain salvation through our Lord Jesus Christ." This is love. God loved us so much that He gave His only begotten Son to die for us— the only Son who came from Him. Now we are saved from His wrath and have obtained salvation.

Remember, God hates sin and John 3:36 shows that His wrath still exists toward all who do not receive His grace: "He who believes in the Son has everlasting life; and he who does not believe the Son shall not see life, but the wrath of God abides on him." However, if we are "in Christ," then Christ's blood covers us, because Jesus took the Father's wrath for us.

Take a look at the words of the Apostle Paul, who certainly knew the love of God and wrote powerfully about it in Romans 8:35, 38- 39:

> Who shall separate us from the love of Christ? Shall tribulation, or distress, or persecution, or famine, or nakedness, or peril, or sword?... For I am persuaded that neither death nor life, nor angels nor principalities nor powers, nor things present nor things to come, nor height nor depth, nor any created thing, shall be able to separate us from the love of God which is in Christ Jesus our Lord.

Truly, the Cross represents God's awesome love for us. Jesus demonstrated this love for us in going to the Cross to die for our sins so we could be joined to God and restored to intimate fellowship with Him. This love, the love of the Father, will transform our lives if we will truly receive it.

Romans 8:32 asks an important question: "[God] did not spare His own Son, but delivered Him up for us all, how shall He not with Him also freely give us all things?" Let's think about this for a moment. If God did not spare His own Son but in fact gave Him and delivered Him to be crucified, to take our sin and punishment, will He not give us everything we need, especially His love? Of course He will!

Over the years, I have prayed for thousands of people and I find that one of the primary issues many people struggle with is simply knowing the love of the Father. Many of these people have received Jesus and may know intellectually that God loves them, but they don't have a revelation of this love in their hearts. This causes all kinds of problems because they are starting from a faulty position of not knowing the Father's love. It is pretty hard to really believe that God wants to answer your prayers and meet your needs if you think He is angry with you.

John 16:27 tells us that the Father Himself loves us, because we have loved the Son. Then in John 17:26 Jesus prays that the love that God had and has for Him would be in us. I believe God answered and will continue to answer Jesus's prayer.

Let me say again that God is not angry with you. He put His wrath on Jesus. Yes, He hates sin, but He loves us. He demonstrated His love in that while we were still sinners Jesus died for us.

What an awesome God! He is love; and He loves us so much.

A Prayer for You

The Apostle Paul, through the inspiration of the Holy Spirit, knew that we needed to know the love of God. As you pray this prayer, from Ephesians 3, believe that the Father wants to answer this prayer for you. That is the reason that He put it in the Bible for us today. He knows we need a revelation of His love in our inner man.

For this reason I bow my knees to the Father of our Lord Jesus Christ, from whom the whole family in heaven and earth is named, that He would grant you, according to the riches of His glory, to be strengthened with might through His Spirit in the inner man, that Christ may dwell in your hearts through faith; that you, being rooted and grounded in love, may be able to comprehend with all the saints what is the width and length and depth and height—to know the love of Christ which passes knowledge; that you may be filled with all the fullness of God. Now to Him who is able to do exceedingly abundantly above all that we ask or think, according to the power that works in us, to Him be glory in the church by Christ Jesus to all generations, forever and ever. Amen.

Ephesians 3:14-21

Take a moment to look at this image of the cross. Christ's death reveals the love of the father described in the passage above. Every time you see a Cross, or anything that resembles a Cross, I pray you will be reminded of how much God loves you!

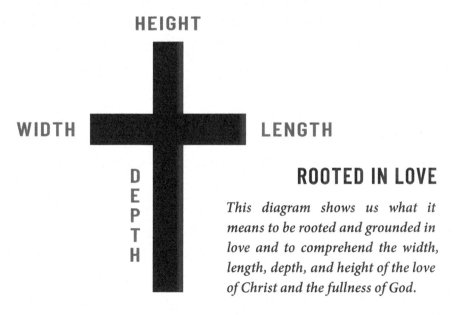

HEIGHT

WIDTH

LENGTH

DEPTH

ROOTED IN LOVE

This diagram shows us what it means to be rooted and grounded in love and to comprehend the width, length, depth, and height of the love of Christ and the fullness of God.

SUMMARY

† The first key to appropriating the power and provision of the Cross is really being established in the Father's intimate, personal, overwhelming love for you.

† God is love. Love is His very essence.

† God is not angry with you but loves you and desires to have relationship with you.

† God has wrath because of sin. Jesus appeased the wrath of God (made propitiation) and reconciled us to God.

† If we are in Christ, His blood covers us. This means that God does not see us as sinners, but as righteous.

How Do We Experience God's Love?

I believe that knowing and experiencing the love of the Father is one of the most life-transforming experiences a person can have. It comes by revelation. If we will ask the Father, He will reveal His love to us, and it will satisfy the greatest need that we have.

We were created in love because the Scripture says we were created in the image and likeness of God (see Gen. 1:26- 27). If this is true, and it is, then we were created in love, because God is love. He really wants to reveal His love to us.

There are various ways we can help ourselves receive the love of the Father. They include renewing our minds according to God's Word; receiving and fully embracing the Holy Spirit; realizing that our earthly fathers do not perfectly reflect or represent our heavenly Father; and obeying God's commandment to forgive.

First and foremost, to experience the love of the Father, we must see what Scripture says about the love of the Father, the love He has demonstrated for us through Jesus and the Cross. This is what we have been doing in discussing the various Scripture references in the previous chapters. In the Appendix of this book, you will find many of the Scriptures that speak of God's love and of the power of the Cross. I encourage you to take time to read and meditate on them.

God's Word is truth; and as we know and abide in the truth, the truth will make you free (see John 8:31- 32). Since the truth makes you free, then a lie will keep you in bondage. If you believe God is angry with you, which is a lie, this will hold you in bondage. If you believe you are unworthy of God's love, this too will keep you in bondage. Do you see the way that the enemy could use lies to place you in bondage and make you unable to receive God's truth? Therefore, you must discover and believe the truth of God's Word to be able to receive the love of the Father.

"If you believe God is angry with you, which is a lie, this will hold you in bondage."

The Word of God is "living" (see Hebrews 4:12), because Jesus is the Word (see Revelation 19:13). By spending time in the Word and especially the Scriptures in this book, faith will rise up in your heart because, "faith comes by hearing and hearing by the word of God" (Romans 10:17).

First John 4:8 declares that God is love. Since He is love, we can begin to gain a more complete revelation of His love by reading from 1 Corinthians 13, which is often called "The Love Chapter" of the Bible. This chapter describes love, but since God is love, I have included His name in my paraphrase of the passage, so you can get a clear picture of the love of the Father.

> Love [God] suffers long. Love [God] is kind; Love [God] does not envy. Love [God] does not parade itself; Love [God] is not puffed up; Love [God] does not behave rudely; Love [God] does not seek its own. Love [God] is not provoked; Love [God] thinks no evil. Love [God] does not rejoice in iniquity; Love [God] rejoices in the truth, Love [God] never fails.
>
> 1 Corinthians 13:4-8

We Must Receive and Fully Embrace the Holy Spirit

It is the Holy Spirit who reveals truth to us (see 1 Corinthians 2:9-12) and leads us into all truth (see John 16:13). It is also the Holy Spirit who pours out the love of God in our hearts (see Romans 5:5); and it is the Holy Spirit, who is the Spirit of Adoption that causes us to cry out, "Abba Father" (see Romans 8:15). Understanding this truth is not a minor issue. The Bible tells us it is the Holy Spirit, who *is* God, who makes the love of God real to us. Without the revelation and illumination the Holy Spirit brings, the love of God will remain primarily an intellectual concept instead of a life-changing reality in our inner being.

"It is The Holy Spirit, who is God, who makes the love of God real to us."

I was raised in a church that did not emphasize the importance of the Holy Spirit and therefore as a young man, I never realized His role in my life. After I was baptized with the Holy Spirit, who is the Promise of the Father for us (see Luke 24:49 and Acts 1:4- 5, 8), I received His love for me. It is the Holy Spirit who continues to reveal the Father's love to me. I know there is much debate about being baptized in the Holy Spirit, but He made all the difference in the world to me.

If you have struggled with this issue, I want to encourage you to do a word study on the Holy Spirit in your Bible. If you do so, you will find so many references to Him and to what He does that it will stagger you. It did me. What I came to discover is that we live in a time referred to as "the last days" and in these last days God is operating by His Spirit.

One day I was reading Luke's account of Jesus being baptized and was amazed by what I found:

> When all the people were baptized, it came to pass that Jesus also was baptized; and while He prayed, the heaven was opened. And the Holy Spirit descended in bodily form like

a dove upon Him, and a voice came from heaven which said, "You are My beloved Son; in You I am well pleased."

Luke 3:21-22

I had read this passage many times before, but this particular experience with it revealed several things to me in a fresh way. The first thing I saw when I read the passage that time was the Holy Spirit came upon Jesus after He was baptized in water. Now, Jesus did not need to be born again by the Holy Spirit. He was born of the Spirit in the first place and had no sin in Him. He became sin for us as we have already seen, but Jesus was not born in sin.

Why would the Holy Spirit come upon Him at His baptism? He did so to release the love of the Father and to empower Him to carry out His mission. It is the same reason we need the Holy Spirit to come upon us. We need the power that comes only from the Holy Spirit to do the things that He is calling us to do. This is why I say we need to fully embrace and receive the Holy Spirit if we are truly going to know the love of the Father.

Let me ask you a question: Did Jesus need the affirmation of the Father? Obviously, in His divinity He did not need that. But in His humanity, He needed the affirmation of the Father. If Jesus needed His Father's love and affirmation, how much more do we need it?

We desperately need to know the love of the Father and receive His affirmation for us. That love and affirmation is what I received when I was baptized in the Holy Spirit. The love of the Father was no longer just some teaching but a revelation from God the Father that I experienced deep in my inner man.

Now you can see why it is so important for us to receive the Holy Spirit, just as Jesus did. The Holy Spirit is the "Spirit of Adoption" (Romans 8:15) and it is the Holy Spirit who reveals the love of the

Father to us (see Romans 5:5). He makes this love from God our Father real to us.

As I continued to read in Luke 4, I was shocked at what I saw:

> Then Jesus, being filled with the Holy Spirit, returned from the Jordan and was led by the Spirit into the wilderness, being tempted for forty days by the devil. And in those days He ate nothing, and afterward, when they had ended, He was hungry. And the devil said to Him, "If You are the Son of God, command this stone to become bread."
>
> Luke 4:1-3

In Luke 4:3, the devil questioned and challenged the word of the Father, which we just read about in Luke 3:22. He said, *"If you are the Son of God ..."* The real issue is not that the devil wanted Jesus to turn stones into bread, but that the devil challenged the Father's love and affirmation of Jesus. Can you imagine this scene? Forty days before this encounter, the Holy Spirit came upon Jesus and the Father spoke from heaven and told Jesus that He was His Beloved Son and that He was well pleased with Him. The devil challenged and questioned the word of the Father concerning His love and affirmation of the Son.

When I saw this, I realized why the love of the Father is such an important issue. The devil hates us; he does not want us to know the love of the Father; and he does not want us to receive His affirmation. Now, if the devil challenged and questioned the direct word of God to the Son, how much more will He challenge and question us in the same way? Since the devil attacked Jesus in this area of the love and affirmation of the Father, I can assure you that he will attack you and me in the same way. We need to be established in the truth of the Word so we can stand against him.

We Must Develop a True and Accurate Image of God

Regardless of what kind of earthly father you had, he is not your heavenly Father. We all have a tendency to project our earthly father's image onto our heavenly Father. Therefore, most of us have a faulty image of God even if our fathers were great.

The following chart demonstrates different relationships we may have had with our parents and how we may mistakenly view God as a result of how we view our parents.

As you can see from the chart, depending on what kind of father you had, subconsciously you may think our heavenly Father will treat you the same way. I have prayed for many people who really struggle with this concept. They will agree with me that God is love and that He loves them, but many times they still have a hard time relating to their heavenly Father. This is especially true when their earthly father abused them in any of the ways mentioned in the chart.

The reality that our view of God is affected by the experiences we have had with our earthly fathers is one reason the devil attacks the family, especially fathers. If the devil can corrupt the father, not only is the father hurt, but so is everyone else in the family. He wants to destroy and bring death to everyone, and if his attack is successful on the fathers, it makes it so hard later on in life for us to receive the love of *the* Father.

To break free from this problem of projecting your image of your own dad onto God, ask the Lord to show you if you have any judgments and/or situations of unforgiveness in your heart toward your earthly father. If you do, you must repent of your judgments, release your father and forgive him for everything he did or didn't do in your life.

BEHAVIOR OF PARENT	MISCONCEPTION ABOUT GOD
1. Legalistic • harsh disciplinarians	1. God is mad • authoritarian • impersonal • demanding
2. Perfectionistic • extremely high goals • little praise or affirmation	2. God is never satisfied • always disappointed and upset with me
3. Little or no affection	3. God is impersonal, distant
4. Critical • verbally abusive	4. God is angry • He puts up with people but doesn't really love them
5. Workaholic • focus away from children and outside of the home	5. God is detached and uncaring • it is difficult to get God's attention • I'm really not important to Him
6. Abusive • dominating	6. God rules by fear • even though I may have to obey Him, I don't really trust Him
7. Moody • temperamental	7. God is unpredictable • one day He loves me, the next day He is angry and threatening
8. Sinful • immoral • low standard of discipline and behavior	8. God doesn't mean what He says • God is extremely gracious and is a pushover • no need to fear Him
9. Smothering • doting • spoiling you and never saying no	9. God exists for me • the only thing that matters is my world • God must conform to my needs and desires
10. Had favorite children • compared you with siblings and others	10. God has favorites • He loves "good people" more than sinners • He loves me based on my performance
11. Made promises and broke them • gave warnings and didn't follow through	11. God is unreliable and unfaithful • difficult to believe His Word
12. Were hypocritical • lived one way at home and another way in public	12. God isn't powerful or relevant • religion is for social and special purposes • doesn't relate to my life

*Evans, Jimmy and Ann Billington. *Freedom From Your Past*. Amarillo, TX: Majestic Media, 1994, 2006, pp. 130-131 (Marriage Today, www.marriagetoday.org)

Next, you need the Holy Spirit to heal the hurts and disappointments you may have received from your earthly father. In John 14:9 Jesus says that if you have seen Him you have seen the Father. Therefore, if you want to know what the Father is like, look at Jesus. It is vital that you replace any faulty image you may have of God with the correct image of who He is. One way to do this is to read all four Gospels, which will give you an accurate look at who Jesus is, and therefore, who the Father is. According to Colossians 1:15, Jesus "is the image of the invisible God, the firstborn over all creation." And according to Hebrews 1:3, God's Son is, "the brightness of His glory and the express image of His person."

Remember, Jesus said, "He who has seen Me has seen the Father" (John 14:9). We can picture Jesus as we read about Him walking on the earth, healing people, and then dying for us on the Cross.

God is not like your earthly father. He is God. He is love and He is always a good Father!

We Have to Forgive, Forgive, Forgive

The Bible tells us the greatest command is to love the Lord with all of your heart, soul, mind and strength and to love your neighbor as yourself (Matthew 22:37-40). In John 13:34- 35, Jesus speaks of a new commandment, that we are to love one another as Jesus loves us. Then in 1 John 4:20, we read that if we say we love God but hate our brother, we are liars.

The reason this is so important is that God is love and since He lives in us, He wants us to love also. By not loving our earthly fathers or anyone else, we limit our ability to receive God's love for us. In fact, forgiving one another is one of the greatest expressions of love there is.

Remember, there are two parts to the Cross. The vertical shaft of the Cross represents the love the Father has for us, coming down from heaven. There is no restriction to His love, as we have already seen. However, the other part of the Cross is the horizontal beam, which represents our love for others. God's love is first, but if we want to continue to live and experience His love on an ongoing basis, we must love one another.

We must forgive our earthly fathers and release all judgments that we might have against them because this empowers us to love others as the Lord wants us to love them. Releasing every judgment we hold against our earthly fathers enables us to extend love to others!

SUMMARY

† Receiving the love of the Father is the most life-changing experience you can ever have.

† Receiving the love of the Father is not a one-time event, but an ongoing revelation. To really receive His love, you need to:

> Be assured from Scripture that He really loves you and is for you, not against you.

> Fully embrace the Holy Spirit who reveals the love of the Father to you.

> Deal with any misconceptions of God that you may have from your relationship with your earthly father.

> Allow the Holy Spirit to heal any hurts that may be rooted in your relationship with your parents.

> Forgive and choose to love one another. *Love is a choice, not an emotion.*

Maturing in Christ

Once we begin to understand God's awesome love for us and Jesus's great sacrifice for us on the Cross, we can begin to mature in Christ. Spiritual growth takes place in at least three stages, or levels of revelation:

> "I write to you, *little children,* because your sins are forgiven you for His name's sake. I write to you, *fathers,* because you have known Him who is from the beginning. I write to you, *young men,* because you have overcome the wicked one. I write to you, *little children,* because you have known the Father. I have written to you, *fathers,* because you have known Him who is from the beginning. I have written to you, *young men,* because you are strong, and the word of God abides in you, and you have overcome the wicked one."
>
> 1 John 2:12-14, (emphasis added)

All of us begin in Christ as little children. We then grow into what John calls, "young men," which applies to both men and women. Finally, we gain a measure of spiritual maturity, which John refers to as being a "father," which again applies to both men and women. As you read through this chapter, examine your own life and determine where you are in this progression. This is the first step toward growing into everything God has created you to be.

Little Children

According to 1 John 2:12-14, little children in Christ learn their sins are forgiven. This is the foundational work of the Cross: Jesus died for our sins and we are totally forgiven forever. Our sins are blotted out, erased and forever forgotten by the Lord. Though total forgiveness is a reality, we must grow in our understanding of it, just as little children have to grow in their ability to understand things.

When we have the revelation of what forgiveness really means, we no longer feel guilty, ashamed or condemned. God made a *choice* to forgive us. This Scripture reminds us of how thoroughly and freely we are forgiven: "In Him we have redemption through His blood, the forgiveness of sins, according to the riches of His grace" (Ephesians 1:7).

Vine's Expository Dictionary defines *redemption* as: "a releasing, for payment of a ransom." Our redemption is a finished work. Because we were born in sin, there was a penalty, a death sentence, on us. When Jesus died on the Cross, He took our death certificates and marked them, "paid in full."

"Eternal redemption" is forever (Hebrews 9:12). Our redemption was purchased for the rest of our lives through the blood of Jesus when He forgave our sins. We do not have to wait for God to do anything else, and He is not waiting for us to do anything except receive His gift through faith. Read the verses below and think about how awesome Jesus's sacrifice was. If the blood of goats and calves was able to atone for sins for an entire year, how effective can we believe the blood of the Son of God to be?

> But Christ came as High Priest of the good things to come, with the greater and more perfect tabernacle not made with hands, that is, not of this creation. Not with the blood of goats and calves, but with His own blood He entered the Most Holy Place once for all, having obtained

eternal redemption. For if the blood of bulls and goats and the ashes of a heifer, sprinkling the unclean, sanctifies for the purifying of the flesh, how much more shall the blood of Christ, who through the eternal Spirit offered Himself without spot to God, cleanse your conscience from dead works to serve the living God?

Hebrews 9:11-14

This passage in Hebrews 9 is written in the past tense. The phrase, "having obtained eternal redemption" means this took place at the Cross. It is a done deal. Jesus presented Himself to the Father in Heaven. Jesus entered as the High Priest but offered *Himself* as the sacrifice instead of a bull or a goat. His sinlessness and spotlessness covers our sin completely and forever.

At this stage of growth, we should learn to receive complete forgiveness and cleansing from our past sins. The blood of Christ really does cleanse us. Let's further examine our forgiveness as we look at the difference between guilt and shame.

The late author Ann Billington wrote:

Guilt is a response to something you have done; it is a reaction to your behavior. Perhaps you have sinned, committed an offense, or violated a relationship, and you deeply regret your action. These situations usually generate guilt which leads to one of two responses – condemnation or conviction. If guilt becomes unhealthy, it develops into feelings of condemnation.

Shame, though frequently confused with guilt, condemnation, and conviction, is different. Unlike guilt, shame is not a response to something you have done, but a

> *response to who and what you perceive yourself to be …*
> *Shame is actually the energy behind feelings of inferior-*
> *ity, which entice us to compare ourselves with others.*
> *Shame is an inner sensing of defectiveness that colors*
> *our emotions and relationships and drives us toward*
> *self-deprecating behavior.*
>
> Jimmy Evans and Ann Billington: *Freedom From Your Past,* ©
> 1994, 2006, pp. 141-143 (Marriage Today, www.marriagetoday.org)

There is a difference between guilt and shame. Guilt says, "You did something wrong" but shame says, "You are faulty." Guilt may be a fact; shame is a feeling. Being convicted of wrongdoing by the awareness of your guilt is a good and healthy thing but feeling condemned and living under the burden of the guilt is not. However, shame is a real problem. When people feel shame, they are receiving the lies of the enemy instead of the grace of Christ's death on the Cross, which covers all sin and shame.

Do you still carry guilt and shame from your past? If so, receive the complete forgiveness that Jesus paid for with His blood.

"When we know our sins are forgiven, we are not sin-conscious anymore. Instead, we are righteousness-conscious."

Through Jesus's atoning death on the Cross, God literally made us righteous. We have nothing to be ashamed of because Jesus took all of our sin away from us and took it to the Cross. He actually became sin for us, as 2 Corinthians 5:21 reminds us: "For He made Him who knew no sin to be sin for us, that we might become the righteousness of God in Him."

When we know our sins are forgiven, we are not *sin-conscious* anymore. Instead, we become *righteousness-conscious*. We walk in victory because we are so aware of the power of life that is ours through the death, burial and resurrection of Jesus Christ. He made us righteous through His work on the Cross. Changing the way we think is what repentance is all about.

If you are focused on sin and how bad you are, you have not fully appropriated this truth into your life. Once we are forgiven and cleansed from our sin and our sinful way of life, we become conscious of His love and forgiveness. As long as you see yourself as a sinner, you continue to put that guilt and shame onto yourself. But once you begin to see yourself as a saint, you can walk in the freedom Christ purchased for you on the Cross. I hear so many people say, "Oh, I'm just an ol' sinner saved by grace." But the reality is that you are no longer a sinner, your sins are covered by the blood of Christ and you walk alongside Him—fully forgiven, cleansed by His sacrifice—and you are a saint. This should cause you to rejoice and literally feel clean: no more guilt, no more shame and no more condemnation.

I am not talking about living a sinless life in which we never sin again. What I am talking about is not living in the past and thinking about our past sinful behavior. Allowing your past to define your present is not God's desire for you. His desire is for His Son's life to define your present!

I heard a story about a prophet who was visiting a church one night, prophesying over certain individuals. He had been especially accurate, and he was very clear about times and events in people's lives. One of the ladies in attendance that evening had lived a very rough life prior to coming to know Christ. Even after receiving Jesus as her Savior and changing her lifestyle, she was still bothered by the things that she had experienced and choices that she had made still troubled her.

At one point in the meeting, the prophet called on this lady. He started by saying, "I see that you were involved in," and he abruptly stopped. People in the congregation who knew this lady in the auditorium were holding their breath, thinking that surely, he would not say aloud what she had been involved in. The pause seemed like an eternity to those who were there that night. Then the prophet said, "The Lord says, 'I choose not to remember.'" This word from the Lord released the woman from all the guilt and shame she still carried around because of her past life.

Isn't God good? He *chooses not to remember your sin.* Perhaps you need to hear the same thing in your life. If you have received Jesus, *you are forgiven!* The Lord chooses not to remember your sin any longer. Believe it and receive His love! If you haven't asked for forgiveness, ask now and you can receive forgiveness and cleansing. If you are still walking in some sin, do not remain any longer in guilt and shame; repent and receive forgiveness from it.

Young Men

Remember that 1 John 2:14 says: "I have written to you, young men, because you are strong, and the word of God abides in you, and you have overcome the wicked one." John is saying that in order to be strong in Christ and overcome the wicked one, the Word of God must abide, or dwell continually, in us. When His Word is in our hearts and minds to this degree a maturing process takes place, and we grow from spiritual children into young men. The Word of God brings strength, stability and maturity in ways that nothing else can or will.

As we grow, we begin to realize that we are not only forgiven, but we are also justified. *Justification* is the "legal and formal acquittal from guilt by God as Judge, the pronouncement of the sinner as righteous who believes on the Lord Jesus Christ" (from *Vine's Expository Dictionary*). The process of justification includes being redeemed, forgiven, cleansed and made the righteousness of God. Romans 3:24-26 speaks about our justification:

> Being justified freely by His grace through the redemption that is in Christ Jesus, whom God set forth as a propitiation by His blood, through faith, to demonstrate His righteousness, because in His forbearance God had passed over the sins that were previously committed, to demonstrate at the present time His righteousness, that He might be just and the justifier of the one who has faith in Jesus.
>
> Romans 3:24-26

Romans 3:24-26 contains a lot of words we don't use often: *justification, redemption, propitiation, and forbearance.* The passage almost sounds like several attorneys during a trial—and the only one who understands them is the judge. That image isn't far from the truth. We are being represented by Christ before God (the Judge) and He fully understands what we are only beginning to understand. He knows and sees the fullness of these words and how they apply to each of our cases. Even though these are words we do not use in everyday speech, they are very important. They communicate an even greater depth of meaning to the act that Christ committed at the Cross. These words articulate truths and realities that the words *sacrifice, saved,* and *forgiven* cannot fully convey.

These words are so rich that I want to take a moment to explain them so you can better understand what the Lord has done for us. When we are *justified*, we are legally and formally acquitted of guilt. That means we can stand before God as though we never sinned at all. *Propitiation* means the wrath of God, against the sins of the world, was completely transferred and put upon Jesus at the Cross. Jesus took God's wrath, by shedding His blood, so we could be restored in our relationship with God. *Forbearance* means that God has patiently delayed His judgment and wrath against sin, giving each of us the opportunity to turn from our sin, put our faith in Jesus so we could be justified in Him.

"When we are reconciled to God, we are brought into intimate friendship with Him."

In addition to being forgiven and justified, we are also reconciled to God through the Cross. To be *reconciled* means, "to be changed from enmity to friendship; to reconcile" (*Vine's*). When we are reconciled to God, we are brought into intimate relationship, literally into friendship, with God. This friendship with God is our rightful place—not because of anything we do, but because of what Jesus has already done. We can have peace and intimate friendship with God because of the blood of the Cross. Colossians 1:19- 20 says: "It pleased the Father that in Him all the fullness should dwell and by Him to reconcile all things to Himself, by Him, whether things on earth or things in Heaven, having made peace through the blood of His Cross."

The fact that we are now friends of God is amazing. I previously talked about how many of us think God is angry with us. I hope this will correct our thinking. Not only is God not angry with us, He actually calls us His friends. God has forgiven us and brought us into His family.

More than just being forgiven, we are now "in Christ" and we are righteous before God. Let's look at some more verses together that can help us to understand what it means to be reconciled to God and to be in Christ.

"Now all things are of God, who has reconciled us to Himself through Jesus Christ, and has given us the ministry of rec- onciliation, that is, that God was in Christ reconciling the world to Himself, not imputing their trespasses to them, and has committed to us the ministry of reconciliation."

2 Corinthians 5:18- 19

"But God demonstrates His own love toward us, in that while we were still sinners, Christ died for us. Much more then, having now been justified by His blood, we shall be saved from wrath through Him. For if when we were enemies we were reconciled to God through the death of His Son, much more, having been reconciled, we shall be saved by His life."

Romans 5:8-10 (emphasis added)

God has so much more for us than we are currently experiencing! I see very few people who are walking in the "much more" that Paul is referring to here in Romans and in other passages of Scripture. I believe Paul knew this "much more" that he spoke about and the abundance of all Jesus paid for at the Cross.

This "much more" is referred to throughout Paul's writings. He uses the words "in Him" and "in Christ" when he writes about our being sons or children of God. As we grow into maturity, becoming young men and women in the Lord, we discover a place of favor with God.

Look at the following passages of Scripture and see your position "in Him" and "in Christ."

Blessed be the God and Father of our Lord Jesus Christ, who has blessed us with every spiritual blessing in the heavenly places **in Christ**, just as He chose us in Him before the foundation of the world, that we should be holy and without blame before Him in love, having predestined us to adoption as sons by Jesus Christ **to Himself**, according to the good pleasure of His will, to the praise of the glory of His grace, by which He has made us accepted in the Beloved. **In Him** we have redemption through His blood, the forgiveness of sins, according to the riches of His grace which He made to abound toward us in all wisdom and prudence, having made known to us the mystery of His will, according to His good pleasure which He purposed **in Himself**, that in the dispensation of the fullness of the times He might gather together in one all things **in Christ**, both which are in heaven and which are on earth—**in Him. In Him** also we have obtained an inheritance, being predestined according to the purpose of Him who works all things according to the counsel of His will, that we who first trusted in Christ should be to the praise of His glory. **In Him** also you trusted, after you heard the word of truth, the gospel of your salvation; in whom also, having believed, you were sealed with the Holy Spirit of promise.

Ephesians 1:3-13, (emphasis added)

for **in Him** we live and move and have our being ...

Acts 17:28, (emphasis added)

There is therefore now no condemnation to those who are **in Christ Jesus**.

Romans 8:1, (emphasis added)

Now thanks be to God who always leads us in triumph **in Christ**, and through us diffuses the fragrance of His knowledge in every place."

2 Corinthians 2:14, (emphasis added)

Therefore, if anyone is **in Christ**, he is a new creation; old things have passed away; behold, all things have become new.

2 Corinthians 5:17, (emphasis added)

For He made Him who knew no sin to be sin for us, that we might become the righteousness of God **in Him.**

2 Corinthians 5:21, (emphasis added)

But God, who is rich in mercy, because of His great love with which He loved us, even when we were dead in trespasses, made us alive together with Christ (by grace you have been saved), and raised us up together, and made us sit together in the heavenly places **in Christ Jesus,** that in the ages to come He might show the exceeding riches of His grace in His kindness toward **us in Christ Jesus.**

Ephesians 2:4-7, (emphasis added)

For **in Him** dwells all the fullness of the Godhead bodily; and you are complete **in Him,** who is the head of all principality and power. **In Him** you were also circumcised with the circumcision made without hands, by putting off the body of the sins of the flesh, by the circumcision of Christ."

Colossians 2:9-11, (emphasis added)

These passages show us our true identity, which is "in Him" and "in Christ." We are who God says we are; our identity is not based on what we do or have been. Sometimes we allow our past to define who we are (being called, "a failure," "loser," "stupid," etc.). We even allow the good things in our past to define us. But what we need the most is to discover our true identity as His sons and daughters but also as friends. We have been forgiven and brought into His family. There is no higher position than this.

If we are really going to become the "young men" the Apostle John writes of, we need to be strong in the Word and overcome the wicked one. The only way to do this is by and through the Word of God.

Jesus Himself demonstrated how this works during His encounter with the devil when He was in the wilderness for forty days. In Matthew 4:4, the devil challenged Jesus about being the Son of God and tempted Him to turn stones into bread. Jesus responded from Scripture by quoting Deuteronomy 8:3 saying, "It is written, Man shall not live by bread alone, but by every word that proceeds from the mouth of God."

If Jesus overcame the devil by quoting the Word, then we must do the same.

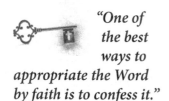

"One of the best ways to appropriate the Word by faith is to confess it."

One of the best ways to appropriate the Word by faith is to confess it. Romans 10:17 says, "Faith comes by hearing, and hearing by the word of God." The best place to hear the Word of God is out of your own mouth! The Word of God is alive and powerful. Learn to incorporate it into every aspect of your life. Read it aloud, memorize it, stop and meditate on a particular verse or passage that seems to "jump" off the page at you. Your faith will be strengthened as you grow in God through His Word.

The word, *meditate* means, "to reflect, to moan, to mutter, to ponder" (from the *Spirit-Filled Life Bible*). It literally means to speak the word over and over, thinking about it and reflecting upon it. Biblical meditation is a very proactive engagement of the mind and helps us get the Word into us. This is what Romans 10:17 means when it says that faith comes by hearing and hearing comes by the Word.

> Blessed is the man who walks not in the counsel of the ungodly, nor stands in the path of sinners, nor sits in the seat of the scornful; but his delight is in the law of the Lord, and in His law he meditates day and night. He shall be like a tree planted by the rivers of water, that brings forth its

fruit in its season, whose leaf also shall not wither; and whatever he does shall prosper.

Psalms 1:1-3

If we will meditate on the Word of God, we will be blessed—like trees planted by the streams of water—yielding fruit and in whatever we do, we will prosper.

Becoming a "Father"

The Lord is longing for us to grow up into everything that He has created and called us to be. Going back to 1 John 2:13- 14, when John writes about "fathers," he is referring to believers who have gained a place of maturity in Christ and are able to express the life of Christ to the people around them. John says that fathers "have known Him who is from the beginning." John is saying that "fathers" are mature believers, men and women, who know God and are walking in their position as both a child of God and as experienced believers.

"Fathers" are mature believers, men or women, who know God."

Our goal is to walk in the position God has for us. We are told in 1 Corinthians 4:15 that we have many instructors but not many fathers. We need fathers and mothers in the Lord who know they are forgiven and have discovered their position as children of God and have continued to grow up in Christ, continually increasing in maturity.

This position is not one of perfection, where we never sin again, but it is a position of living in the love of the Father and becoming sensitive to the promptings of the Holy Spirit. It is a position of really *knowing* God, not just knowing *about* Him.

During the "young man" stage, we discover who we are "in Christ." Then in the "father" stage, we discover who He is in us! This transition from "child of God" to "young man" to "father" brings us into the fullness of who God created us to be.

In Colossians 1:24-26, the Apostle Paul tells us of his calling to preach the Word as a minister of the Gospel. He said he was called to declare the mystery or hidden truth that has now been revealed. That mystery is "Christ in you, the hope of glory."

Paul goes on further in Colossians 1 to explain how we transition into this "father" stage:

> To them God willed to make known what are the riches of the glory of this mystery among the Gentiles: which is Christ in you, the hope of glory. Him we preach, warning every man and teaching every man in all wisdom, that we may present every man perfect in Christ Jesus.
>
> Colossians 1:27- 28

Not only are you "in Christ," but as you grow into the father stage you will really discover what it means to have "Christ in you." Knowing Christ is in you causes you to become God-conscious, not focused on what you have done right or done wrong, but on your relationship with Him. Let me say that again: God is all about relationship. He wants you to know Him and love Him with all your heart.

God loves each of us with all of His heart and He wants us to be passionate lovers of Him. At this stage, that of a "father," we are not concerned with rules and regulations but with our relationship with Him. It is not that the rules no longer apply; but, at this stage, if we do things or have an attitude that hurts our relationship with God, the Holy Spirit lovingly prompts us to change. This "father" stage is all about a loving relationship with God the Father and with one another. People who are "fathers" will reveal God the Father in their lives and actions. This is what was needed in Paul's time, and is still needed today.

Look What Jesus Has Done!

We have been redeemed by the blood of Jesus—and completely forgiven. The penalty for our sin has been paid in full, and we have been released from bondage and the penalty of death. Jesus literally became sin with our sinfulness so that we could become the righteousness of God. This is the process of justification, which is the legal term we talked about before, meaning, "to be formally acquitted."

We are redeemed!

We are forgiven!

We are righteous!

We are justified!

But this is not all. We can understand the basic tenets of salvation but still not be experiencing the fullness of what Jesus accomplished at the Cross. Not only did He redeem us, forgive us, make us righteous and justify us, He also reconciled us to God. This reconciliation brings us into a place of intimate friendship, actually becoming a child of God. He adopted us into His family.

> For you did not receive the spirit of bondage again to fear, but you received the Spirit of adoption by whom we cry out, "Abba, Father." The Spirit Himself bears witness with our spirit that we are children of God, and if children, then heirs—heirs of God and joint heirs with Christ, if indeed we suffer with Him, that we also may be glorified together.
> Romans 8:15-17

We have been reconciled to God.

We have been given the Spirit of adoption.

We are children of God.

We are joint heirs with Jesus.

We are now part of the family of God.

SUMMARY

†　There are three basic stages of our Christian walk: the child stage, the young man stage, and the father stage.

†　As little children or new believers, we learn about the foundational work of the Cross—that Jesus died for our sins and we are totally forgiven forever. We learn not to live in the past and not to let our pasts define our present.

†　As young men, we move beyond simply knowing we are forgiven into understanding what it means to be justified—acquitted by God and pronounced righteous. This understanding enables us to see who we are in Christ and to recognize ourselves as God's friends. We also have the passion and discipline to study the Bible and overcome the wicked one by the Word during this stage of our spiritual growth.

†　As fathers, we have matured to the place of knowing our position in Christ, walking in the authority that God has given us, and discovering that not only are we "in Christ" but He is in us!

†　God is a God of relationships. He wants to know us and to be known by us.

† God loves us passionately and wants that same kind of passion to come from us toward Him.

♥ TAKE IT TO HEART

Take a few moments to think about how you would characterize your level of maturity in Christ. Would you say you are a "child", a "young [wo]man", or a "father"? What are some of the reasons why you believe that? Perhaps the Lord has already spoken to you about the next steps you need to take in order to grow in your spiritual walk. Consider the importance of "abiding in the Word" and make a decision to set aside time on a regular basis to deepen your relationship with the Father and come to know who He is and all that's in His heart for you.

🙏 TAKE IT TO GOD

Dear God,

I am so thankful that You had a plan for my life from the beginning of time and that You will complete and perfect all that's in Your heart for me. I trust that through every stage of this maturing process, You will lead, guide, speak and reveal the paths that I am called to walk. Most importantly, I say, "Yes" to the loving work of Your Spirit in my life and celebrate my forever-sealed relationship with You.

In Jesus's name. Amen.

Part 3

The Exchange of the Cross

"Jesus took from us all of our sin,
our sickness, our brokenness,
our shame and death
and gave us His forgiveness,
His healing, His wholeness
and His abundant life."

Our Inheritance as Heirs of God

Quite possibly, Jesus's death appeared to be the greatest defeat of all time, but it was actually the greatest victory ever known. In fact, at the Cross, Jesus exchanged our death for His life; and He exchanged our every defeat for His victory. What an amazing love!

At the Cross, Jesus took from us all of our sin, our sickness, our brokenness, our shame and death and gave us His forgiveness, His healing, His wholeness and His abundant life. This is what we call "the exchange of the Cross."

In the previous chapter, we discovered who we are as children of God. One of the Scriptures we read was Romans 8:17, "and if children, then heirs—heirs of God and joint heirs with Christ." This promises us that we have received an inheritance! As sons and daughters of God, the exchange of the Cross—and the incredible fullness of everything it means—is our "inheritance" from God our Father. When Jesus died on the Cross, He purchased for us everything we would ever need.

Just as an earthly father often leaves an inheritance to his children upon his death, our heavenly Father has given us an inheritance. This inheritance is made possible by the death of Jesus Christ. Just as an earthly father would have a last will and testament, God has given us His last will and testament in His Word. In fact, the New Testament is His Word regarding our inheritance. Everything He has given us—and the directions for fully enjoying all His benefits—is recorded in the Bible. Just as a person's earthly life must be complete before an inheritance is granted, Jesus's work on the Cross is a finished work that has forever guaranteed our inheritance.

The Scriptures below will help you catch a glimpse of what God has provided for us through the death, burial and resurrection of Jesus Christ:

> Blessed be the God and Father of our Lord Jesus Christ, who has blessed us with every spiritual blessing in the heavenly places in Christ.
>
> Ephesians 1:3

> As His divine power has given to us all things that pertain to life and godliness, through the knowledge of Him who called us by glory and virtue.
>
> 2 Peter 1:3

> In Him also we have obtained an inheritance, being predestined according to the purpose of Him who works all things according to the counsel of His will.
>
> Ephesians 1:11

> Giving thanks to the Father who has qualified us to be partakers of the inheritance of the saints in the light.
>
> Colossians 1:12

Galatians 3:26-29 promises: "For you are all sons of God through faith in Christ Jesus. For as many of you as were baptized into Christ have put on Christ ... And if you are Christ's, then you are Abraham's seed, and *heirs according to the promise*" (emphasis mine).

We become heirs of God through faith in Jesus Christ. All who believe in Christ are children of God and heirs to every promise He has made.

Galatians 4:6 says that we know we are God's children because His Spirit within us cries out, "Abba, Father!" In other words, we know in our hearts that we belong to Him, and that positions us as His heirs.

When Paul writes that we "have put on Christ" in baptism, he is referring to our position "in Christ," with all its benefits. When Paul refers to us as Abraham's seed, we see that we are the beneficiaries of the covenant promises God made to Abraham

"We are the beneficiaries of the covenant promises God made throughout Scriptures."

and then throughout the Scriptures, all the way through the Cross. In fact, as the Bible says in Galatians 3:29 we are "heirs according to the promise." As God's children, we can count on Him to keep every promise He has made.

> But when the fullness of time had come, God sent forth His Son, born of a woman, born under the law, to redeem those who were under the law, that we might receive adoption as sons. And because you are sons, God has sent forth the Spirit of His Son into your hearts, crying out, "Abba, Father!" Therefore you are no longer a slave but a son, and if a son, then an heir of God through Christ.
>
> Galatians 4:4-7

The Ultimate Exchange

The Cross of Jesus Christ represents the most awesome, most unfair exchange in human history. Jesus, the sinless Lamb, took upon Himself all the sin, iniquity and wretchedness of everyone who would ever live. He took all of what we had and exchanged it for what He has. He took our sin, our sickness, our shame, our rejection, our pain and even our death so He could give us His life and all its benefits. The following verses help us understand this:

And you He made alive, who were dead in trespasses and sin ... But God, who is rich in mercy, because of His great love with which He loved us, even when we were dead in trespasses, made us alive together with Christ ... that in the ages to come He might show the exceeding riches of His grace in His kindness toward us in Christ Jesus. For by grace you have been saved through faith, and that not of yourselves; it is the gift of God.

Ephesians 2:1, 4-8

He is despised and rejected by men, a Man of sorrows and acquainted with grief. And we hid, as it were, our faces from Him; He was despised, and we did not esteem Him. Surely He has borne our griefs and carried our sorrows; yet we esteemed Him stricken, smitten by God, and afflicted. But He was wounded for our transgressions, He was bruised for our iniquities; the chastisement for our peace was upon Him, and by His stripes we are healed.

Isaiah 53:3-5

Yet it pleased the Lord to bruise Him; He has put Him to grief. When you make His soul an offering for sin...

Isaiah 53:10

This is amazing! The Father was actually pleased for the Son to go to the Cross and exchange all of our sinfulness for all of His blessings. This chart below helps emphasize so clearly what Christ has done for each one of us.

JESUS...	YOU...
Was punished	Are forgiven
Was made sin	Are made righteous
Was rejected	Are accepted
Was cut off by sin	Are joined to God
Bore your shame	Share His glory
Was wounded	Are healed
Became poor	Share His abundance
Became a curse	Receive blessing
Died our death	Share His life

SUMMARY

† We have an inheritance in the Kingdom of God because of what Jesus did at the Cross. We have everything we need because of His sacrifice.

† We are God's heirs. We are no longer slaves, but sons. This means we have been redeemed and are adopted into His family!

† Jesus was punished, rejected, wounded and killed so we could be forgiven, accepted, healed and share in His abundance, life and blessing! That isn't a fair or an even exchange, but we receive a mighty blessing because Christ was willing to make it!

The Great Exchange

Few people seem to walk in the full measure of the victory Christ gained at the Cross. I do not want to be one of them, and I don't believe you want to be one either. I don't want to get to Heaven some-day and find that there was so much more I could have had during my life on earth. God offers us so much, and don't want to miss any of it because I didn't know about it or was unwilling to believe it was available for me. I'm sure you feel the same way.

Jesus has *already* (past tense) paid for all of our sin. When He said, on the Cross, "It is finished," He meant it. Jesus paid with His life for us to possess and live in His victory. In order to experience the fullness of everything God has for us, we need to appropriate the exchange of the Cross into our lives. Let's look at each specific area of the exchange of the Cross, so we can better understand what Jesus did for us.

The **Exchanges of the Cross** include: exchanging our punishment for God's forgiveness; exchanging our sinfulness for His righteous-ness; exchanging our rejection for His acceptance; exchanging our separation from God for His reconciliation; exchanging our shame for His honor and glory; exchanging our pain and sickness for His healing; exchanging our lack for His abundance; exchanging curses for blessings; and exchanging our death for His life.

As we look at each exchange, consider how you can exchange what you are currently experiencing or have known in the past for what Jesus makes available to you now.

Exchanged Punishment for Forgiveness

Jesus was punished so we could be forgiven. He went to the Cross and allowed God the Father to punish Him for our transgressions. The prophet Isaiah spoke some powerful words about Jesus 700 years before the time of Christ. This is a key Scripture that helps us understand the exchange of the Cross:

> He is despised and rejected by men, a Man of sorrows and acquainted with grief. And we hid, as it were, our faces from Him; He was despised, and we did not esteem Him. Surely, He has borne our griefs and carried our sorrows; Yet we esteemed Him stricken, smitten by God, and afflicted. But He was wounded for our transgressions; He was bruised for our iniquities; the chastisement for our peace was upon Him, and by His stripes we are healed.
>
> Isaiah 53:3-5

Let's look at this more carefully. Jesus was wounded for our transgressions and crushed for our iniquities. Why? So we could be forgiven. We have discussed this in previous chapters, but we really need to see Jesus on the Cross, with the Father putting upon Him the punishment we deserved so that we could be forgiven.

"Because of the Cross, we get to exchange our shame for His honor and glory."

Remember the penalty for sin is death. Since we are born in sin the penalty of death was attached to us when we were born. This is the reason we must be born again by the Spirit.

Now let's look again at Colossians 2:13-14:

> And you, being dead in your trespasses and the uncircumcision of your flesh, He has made alive together with Him,

having forgiven you all trespasses, having wiped out the handwriting of requirements that was against us, which was contrary to us. And He has taken it out of the way, having nailed it to the Cross.

This passage of Scripture makes so clear the fact that we were dead in our transgressions, and the penalty of those transgressions was a death sentence upon us. When Jesus went to the Cross, those death certificates that were ours were nailed to the Cross with Him. Through His wonderful act of compassion and mercy, He made us alive with Him and completely forgave us. Now we are reconciled to Him forever.

Can you process what that means to you? The God of all Creation decided to take your suffering, your pain, your condemnation and put it upon His Son at the Cross so you could be forgiven. There should no longer be any residue of guilt. Because of what Jesus did, your nature has been changed; you're a saint, not a sinner. You have the right to intimacy with God, a deep relationship with the Creator of the universe!

The better we understand the magnitude of Jesus's dying on the Cross for us, the greater our love for the Father should be.

Exchanged Sin for Righteousness

Jesus became sin and took our sin upon Himself so we could be made righteous. Second Corinthians 5:21 says, "For He made Him who knew no sin to be sin for us, that we might become the righteousness of God in Him." We are not only forgiven, but He made us righteous. In making us righteous, Jesus cleanses us from sin and the residue of sin so we can stand before God in righteousness.

Our position of righteousness is "in Him." We are not only forgiven, but also made righteous. You might say at this point, "But I am not always righteous; I don't always do what is right." That is true. We sometimes sin, but the provision for our righteousness has already been paid and we have been forgiven. Romans 3 and 4 are all about understanding our righteousness. We can't make ourselves righteous. I won't cover that in its entirety but take the time to read those chapters. You will be glad you did.

"Because of the Cross, we get to exchange our shame for His honor and glory."

The Old Testament includes many Scriptures about righteousness. In Old Testament times the only way to be righteous was to follow the rules, the letter of the Law. But today, our position is a place of grace. Righteousness is now available to us because of the grace poured upon us by the gift of Christ's death on the Cross.

God's Word is clear that we *can* and *do* sin. However, if we confess our sin (which means agreeing with God about our sinful attitudes and actions), He is faithful and just to forgive us and cleanse us from all of our unrighteousness. 1 John 1:8-9 says, "If we say that we have no sin, we deceive ourselves, and the truth is not in us. If we confess our sins, He is faithful and just to forgive us our sins and to cleanse us from all unrighteousness."

God loved us so much that He completely forgave us and made us righteous. He also knew that we could still sin; therefore, He made provision for that too.

Can we earn God's favor? Many times, we try to work and "do good," as if we could ever be good enough to impress God. It is clear that we are to do good works out of our love for Christ, not to earn His favor.

Exchanged Rejection for Acceptance

Jesus was despised and rejected by men so we could be accepted in the beloved (see Is. 53:3; Eph. 1:6). No one has ever been rejected more than Jesus was. Even His disciples left Him when He went to the Cross. He took our rejection and was rejected for us so we could be accepted into the family of God.

Even though we are fully accepted, it still seems that many of us struggle with rejection. Rejection is the absence of real, meaningful love. Even if our parents were wonderful, many of us may still feel rejected at times. We are always looking for and longing to be loved and accepted. When we are young, peer pressure is very strong. We want to be part of what we perceive as the "in" group. The truth is that we are looking for love that is not conditional, but the truth is that unconditional, satisfying love is only found in the Father through the Son. The Father Himself put within us a deep inner need for love and only His love can fulfill it.

God's kind of love is called in Greek *agape*. This word for love is used in the New Testament to describe the unconditional love that God has for us. It was demonstrated in and through Jesus when He went to the Cross to die for us even though we were helpless and dead in our sins. This God-love causes us to break out of rejection and the fear of rejection so we can move into a place of complete acceptance.

Your parents, your brothers and sisters, your friends, your husband or wife and many others may have rejected you, but God has not rejected you. In fact, the Word says that He chose us, and we are now accepted in the Beloved:

> Just as He chose us in Him before the foundation of the world, that we should be holy and without blame before Him in love, having predestined us to adoption as sons by

Jesus Christ to Himself, according to the good pleasure of His will, to the praise of the glory of His grace, by which He has made us accepted in the Beloved.

Ephesians 1:4-6

Will you receive what these verses are saying to you? This passage is life changing: He *chose* us! God chose you before the foundation of the earth. You might say, "My parents didn't want me. I was a mistake, an accident," but God says, "I chose you before time began."

Chosen in Him

Not only did God choose you and me, He has also predetermined that if we accept His choosing, He will adopt us as sons or daughters through Jesus Christ, according to His good pleasure. Again and again, we see that it was God who chose us, forgave us, and has pursued us with His great love.

He predestined us to adoption. Many people ask: "If we were 'predestined' by God to salvation, then why does it matter what we do?"

I believe God has predetermined that if we will receive His offering, He has already predetermined to accept us! If you will receive what He has done, you're in! You're part of the family!

You may have received a pre-approved credit card application in the mail. If you respond to the invitation, you are already approved and will receive credit. However, if you don't respond to the invitation, you cannot access the line of credit being offered to you. Pre-destination works in a similar way; you have to accept the invitation that has already been prepared for you.

Ephesians 1:4-6 goes on to say that we are accepted in the Beloved. "The Beloved" is Jesus and we are accepted because of His blood. Therefore, we are one with Him and He is one with us. We are also one with all the others who choose to be chosen. His acceptance breaks the power of rejection in our lives.

Rejection is one of the meanest spirits and/or mindsets I have ever encountered. Rejection entered the world at the fall; when Satan fell from Heaven, he was rejected. He carried that rejection into the Garden and impacted Adam and Eve negatively, causing them to believe God was withholding something from them.

Our destiny in Christ is all about relationships; everything hinges on relationships. I believe the most important issue people struggle with is knowing the love of the Father. Without knowing His love we experience rejection. Many of us feel rejected by everyone. It doesn't matter what people do or what they say, we still feel rejected. But it is clear from the abundance of Scripture we have already looked at that God is love. He loves us and *we are no longer rejected but accepted.*

You are accepted in the Beloved! This is not so you can be arrogant or prideful, but so you can walk in a pure position of knowing the God of Creation knows you and loves you! You don't have to perform to be accepted. You were already accepted before you did one thing!

If you feel rejection, you may actually be feeling self-rejection, a perverted form of love. We cannot define how people will love us. But we need to *know* His acceptance. Jesus was rejected on the Cross so that you could be accepted!

> *"If you feel rejection, you may actually be feeling self-rejection."*

To help yourself become established in the truth that you are accepted, I encourage you to read the following words aloud: *I am loved by the Father and I am no longer rejected but I have been chosen by God, adopted into the family of God and I am completely accepted in the Beloved. Father please make your love real to me and help me get free from all rejection. Thank you, Jesus. Amen.*

I believe it is time for you to receive God's love, His acceptance, and His choosing completely, regardless of what you have experienced in the past. Remember, His opinion is the only one that counts!

Exchanged Separation from God for Reconciliation

Sin separates people from God. Jesus was literally cut off from the Father by sin, then reconciled so we too could be reconciled to God. Isaiah 53:8 says, "For He was cut off from the land of the living; for the transgressions of My people He was stricken."

On the Cross, Jesus quotes Psalms 22:1, saying, "My God, My God, why have You forsaken Me?" He was forsaken for a brief moment so we could be reconciled to the Father.

What an awesome event! Jesus took our sin upon Himself so we could be restored to relationship with the Father.

> Now all things are of God, who has reconciled us to Himself through Jesus Christ, and has given us the ministry of reconciliation, that is, that God was in Christ reconciling the world to Himself, not imputing their trespasses to them, and has committed to us the word of reconciliation. Now then, we are ambassadors for Christ, as though God were pleading through us: we implore you on Christ's behalf, be reconciled to God.
>
> 2 Corinthians 5:18-20

We are now reconciled to the Father through the Son and we have peace, according to Colossians 1:20- 21: "And by Him to reconcile all things to Himself, by Him, whether things on earth or things in heaven, having made peace through the blood of His Cross. And you, who once were alienated and enemies in your mind by wicked works, yet now He has reconciled."

This reconciliation allows us to be friends of God. Isn't this amazing—the God of the Universe, who created all things, would cause us to be joined to Him in eternal relationship and call us His friends?

Exchanged Shame for Honor

Isaiah 53:3 says Jesus was a Man of sorrows and Isaiah 53:4 says He carried our sorrows. The word *sorrows* could just as easily have been translated *pain*. Jesus literally took our pain. This includes both emotional and physical pain. We experience much emotional pain in this life, but Jesus bore our hurts, our pain and our shame. He took our shame and guilt so we could share in His glory. We have already discussed this in a previous chapter, but He died so that He could literally take our shame and guilt from us.

Hebrews 2:10- 11 says: "For it was fitting for Him, for whom are all things and by whom are all things, in bringing many sons to glory, to make the captain of their salvation perfect through sufferings. For both He who sanctifies and those who are being sanctified are all of one, for which reason He is not ashamed to call them brethren." Because we have been sanctified through His suffering, we will be brought into His glory.

Instead of shame and pain, Jesus has given us double honor. Because of this, we will rejoice and have everlasting joy, according to Isaiah 61:7: "Instead of your shame you shall have double honor, and instead of confusion they shall rejoice in their portion. Therefore in their land they shall possess double; everlasting joy shall be theirs."

Truly, we should be having double portions of His love and mercy. God does not want you to suffer shame and

> *"Being a chosen child of the King is an honor."*

confusion. When the King chooses you, you should feel honored. Shame will cause you to make bad decisions and feel rejected but being a chosen child of the King is an honor.

Have you exchanged your shame for double honor? When you give the Lord all of your sinful past, everything that has caused you to feel ashamed and all the pain associated with it, you will feel clean and you will rejoice and have everlasting joy.

Exchange the shame for His glory. It is time for joy to spring up from your inmost being. Jesus paid for us to have joy. Jesus tells us in John 15:11 that He wants us to have His joy and to be filled with joy. He also says, "Most assuredly, I say to you that you will weep and lament, but the world will rejoice; and you will be sorrowful, but your sorrow will be turned into joy" (John 16:20).

Exchanged Pain and Sickness for Healing

At the Cross, Jesus was severely wounded, taking our pain and sickness so we could be healed. Isaiah 53:3-5 says:

> He is despised and rejected by men, a Man of sorrows and acquainted with grief. And we hid, as it were, our faces from Him; He was despised, and we did not esteem Him. Surely He has borne our griefs and carried our sorrows; yet we esteemed Him stricken, smitten by God, and afflicted. But He was wounded for our transgressions, He was bruised for our iniquities; the chastisement for our peace was upon Him, and by His stripes we are healed.

As mentioned, the Hebrew word for *sorrows* could easily be translated *pain*. The word for *griefs* could have been translated *sickness*. Notice that Isaiah 53:5 says, "by His stripes we are healed." Isaiah was looking forward, toward the Cross and he knew the importance of what would happen at the time of Christ's death. The beatings and scourging Jesus received upon the Cross healed us.

Some people believe this verse refers to spiritual healing alone, not physical healing. That could be true, but the Hebrew word used for *healed* in verse 5 is a word that connotes physical healing and is used throughout the Old Testament. It probably means healing for spirit, soul and body. God always goes way beyond what we think. Why would He limit healing to spiritual matters and leave out the other ways in which we need to be healed? Let's look in the New Testament.

In Matthew 8:16-17, the Holy Spirit reveals through Matthew that Isaiah was referring to both spiritual and physical healing when he wrote Isaiah 53: "When evening had come, they brought to Him many who were demon-possessed. And He cast out the spirits with a word, and healed all who were sick, that it might be fulfilled which was spoken by Isaiah." Matthew understood that Isaiah was looking prophetically forward to the Cross, where Jesus would provide for our healing.

Later in the New Testament, Peter was looking back at the Cross and saw that by Christ's stripes we were healed. He writes: "who Himself bore our sins in His own body on the tree, that we, having died to sins, might live for righteousness—by whose stripes you were healed" (1 Peter 2:24).

That is why Isaiah 53:5, looking toward the Cross, says that by His stripes we *are* healed and 1 Peter 2:24, written after Jesus went to the Cross, says that by His stripes we *were* healed. Our position is with Peter, looking back at the Cross. He tells us that by the work of the Cross, we were healed.

Through Jesus's broken and beaten body, He took our pain, our suffering and our sickness so we could be healed. This is not saying we cannot get sick, but rather that Jesus loved us so much that He made provision for us to be healed.

If you are sick in your body right now, why don't you exchange your sickness for His healing? You can pray and believe for healing for yourself and for others.

Exchanged Lack for Abundance

Jesus became poor so we could share His abundance. The Bible tells us Jesus did not have a place to lay His head; clearly, He did not have many earthly possessions. But there is no lack in Heaven. God uses gold to pave streets. Let's look at what Scripture says about this. In the passage below, Paul says Jesus became poor so we might become rich:

> For you know the grace of our Lord Jesus Christ, that though He was rich, yet for your sakes He became poor, that you through His poverty might become rich.
>
> 2 Corinthians 8:9

Some people believe this Scripture refers not to financial provision, but to spiritual wealth. I believe it is talking about both. Read 2 Corinthians chapters 8 and 9. These chapters are the context for this verse. They are all about finances and the grace of giving money.

Starting with 2 Corinthians 8:1, Paul instructs the people of the church at Corinth to abound in "this grace"—the grace of giving. He is instructing them on the use of their finances, caring for others and stewardship of their resources.

"The Kingdom of God operates out of a different economy from the world."

The world operates according to a different economy than the

Kingdom of God does. In the world, the question is, "how much can I get?" But in the Kingdom, the question is, "How much can I give?"

Provision for everything we need was made at the Cross. Now it does not say He is going to give us a big house on the hill and a new Cadillac. He wants us to have an abundance for every good work. Money itself isn't evil; the love of money is the root of all evil (see 1 Timothy 6:10). God wants to bless and provide for His children.

If you read 2 Corinthians 8:1; 9:15, you will find we have a part to play. We must be rich toward God. Jesus has provided for us based on His unlimited resources. God is a giver. He gave us Jesus, life and love. We should be givers too. We are to be generous, as God is, with our finances, talents, time, and any other resources we have.

I encourage you today: exchange any area where you are lacking for God's abundance.

Exchanged Curses for Blessings

Galatians 3:13-14 says:

> Christ has redeemed us from the curse of the law, having become a curse for us (for it is written, "Cursed is everyone who hangs on a tree"), that the blessing of Abraham might come upon the Gentiles in Christ Jesus, that we might receive the promise of the Spirit through faith.

This is a clear reference to the exchange of the Cross. Jesus took all the curses that are on us so the blessings of Abraham could become ours.

Curses can come to us through our families and many times we continue in them, not even aware that Jesus has redeemed us from the curse. If you see bad fruit from curses coming through your family line to you, recognize it and declare that you don't want it. You have the power in Christ to stop it in your generation. Now this exchange of curses for blessing must be appropriated by faith in our lives. What is the blessing? The blessing is that we have received the Spirit of God. There are blessings in natural things—family relationships, financial blessings, blessings of health and wholeness—all kinds of blessings that God wants for us here and now that have been robbed from us because of curses in our families. God is a generational God. He wants us to understand the dynamics of family generations. He wants to bless us through our family lines so we can receive the blessings of our generations, not the curses.

Exchanged Death for Life

Because of our sin, we deserved death, but Jesus died our death, dying for us so we could have life. We have already looked at many verses that clearly teach that we have been given life. John 3:16 tells us that God so loved us that through Jesus we might have life and in John 10:10, that we might have abundant life. This is talking about life here on earth, now and forever.

Jesus died our death and tasted death for us so we could be released from the fear of death. Hebrews 2:9 says, "But we see Jesus, who was made a little lower than the angels, for the suffering of death crowned with glory and honor, that He, by the grace of God, might taste death for everyone." This does not mean we will not die, but that we do not have to "taste death" because of what Jesus did. It means death won't last forever. We will put off our earthly bodies, but we will be given spiritual bodies. Death is simply a transition into our eternal life. Jesus tasted death for us so we could have life eternal.

Hebrews 2:14- 15 encourages us:

Inasmuch then as the children have partaken of flesh and blood, He Himself likewise shared in the same, that through death He might destroy him who had the power of death, that is, the devil, and release those who through fear of death were all their lifetime subject to bondage.

This passage assures us that we don't need to fear dying. We will get to see the Lord as He really is and be with Him for eternity!

2 Corinthians 5:1-4 says:

For we know that if our earthly house, this tent, is destroyed, we have a building from God, a house not made with hands, eternal in the heavens. For in this we groan, earnestly desiring to be clothed with our habitation which is from heaven, if indeed, having been clothed, we shall not be found naked. For we who are in this tent groan, being burdened, not because we want to be unclothed, but further clothed, that mortality may be swallowed up by life.

Walking in Newness of Life

Jesus was buried so we could be raised to walk in newness of life. 2 Corinthians 5:17 promises: "Therefore, if anyone is in Christ, he is a new creation; old things have passed away; behold, all things have become new." We are new creations in Christ Jesus. The reason we can have life is that Jesus is no longer in the grave. God raised Him from the dead to live forevermore; therefore, because He lives we live too, according to Romans 6:4 "Therefore we were buried with Him through baptism into death, that just as Christ was raised from the dead by the glory of the Father, even so we also should walk in newness of life."

Since He died on the Cross for us and was buried and raised from the dead by the power of God, we are now new creations "in Christ." We are not just "fixed up" or "repaired." We are actually new creations.

If we are heirs, that means we have an inheritance. Having an inheritance means that someone has died. Christ died for us! He died so we could live full of life, full of love, and join Him in His ministry of setting people free and bringing forth the Kingdom of God!

You are righteous. By the blood of Christ, you are made righteous; you are loved and accepted. Look back over the chart in Chapter 6 and start thanking the Lord for all He has done for you. I encourage you to go through the whole list of exchanges, now that you have read more about each one. The goodness of God and His great love revealed to us through Jesus going to the Cross for you and me is awesome. What He has provided for us in the exchange of the Cross is truly amazing.

"Are you ready to receive your inheritance and exchange the pain and brokenness for an abundant life?"

Have you made all of these exchanges? Are you ready to receive your inheritance and exchange all the negative things in your life for the abundant life and victory that Jesus purchased, with His life, on the Cross? Remember: truth will make you free!

To appropriate these exchanges, I suggest you make a copy of the exchange of the Cross and begin to confess these exchanges daily in your prayer time. Keep this chart close and available to you to remind you of all Jesus did for you at the Cross, which is truly the key to everything.

SUMMARY

† Jesus was punished so you could be forgiven

† Jesus was made sin so you could be made righteous

† Jesus was rejected so you would be accepted

† Jesus was cut off by death and you are now joined to God

† Jesus bore your shame and you now share in His glory

† Jesus was wounded and you are healed

† Jesus became poor so you could share in His abundance

† Jesus became a curse, dying on a tree, so you could receive His blessing

† Jesus died our death that we deserved because of sin, and now we have the freedom to share in His life!

♥ TAKE IT TO HEART

Take a few moments to consider the weight of the sacrifice and the love of God for you. Not only did He allow His only begotten Son to be the exchange, the propitiation, and the payment for the sins of the world, but He also made provision (promises) that would bring us freedom, healing, abundance and blessings, righteousness, acceptance, and so much more. His great love is that magnificent and His desire is for you to become a joint heir in every promise He has made. Ask yourself, and ask God to show you in what ways have you have already received this exchange of the Cross of Christ? Is there more fulfillment that you can step into? Are there more of His promises waiting for you?

TAKE IT TO GOD

Dear God,

I come to You in the name of Jesus and I ask for Your forgiveness for all of the things I have done to offend You or hurt others. I acknowledge the costly price that Jesus paid for me, and I accept the exchange He made on the Cross that started my new life in Christ.

In my acceptance of this exchange, I not only cast my cares upon You, but ask You to exchange my heart for Your heart, my will for Your will, and my desires for Your desires. Thank you for the blessings, promises and inheritance that are mine because of Your great love.

In Jesus's name. Amen.

The Essence of Faith

But without faith it is impossible to please Him, for he who comes to God must believe that He is, and that He is a rewarder of those who diligently seek Him.

Hebrews 11:6

We receive the work of the Cross by faith and only by faith. Once we know what God has given us through His Son, we must apprehend that provision by faith. Any inheritance is based on promises, and God's Word is His promise to us. We must trust Him to fulfill every promise He has made toward us and believe that, "He who promised is faithful" (Hebrews 10:23).

Let's focus on God's promises for a moment. One of the exchanges that occurred at the Cross has to do with receiving the blessing of Abraham. Let's look at Hebrews 6:12-20 so we can see how Abraham received his blessing:

> That you do not become sluggish but imitate those who through faith and patience inherit the promises. For when God made a promise to Abraham, because He could swear by no one greater, He swore by Himself, saying, "Surely blessing I will bless you, and multiplying I will multiply you." And so, after he had patiently endured, he obtained the promise.
>
> Hebrews 6:12-15

We see here that we inherit a promise through faith and patience. Abraham had to endure and wait patiently to receive his promise. How can we do this? When everything in life screams at us and tells us good things are not going to happen, we need to exhibit patience and trust that He will keep His Word and fulfill His promises.

> For men indeed swear by the greater, and an oath for confirmation is for them an end of all dispute. Thus God, determining to show more abundantly to the heirs of promise the immutability of His counsel, confirmed it by an oath, that by two immutable things, in which it is impossible for God to lie, we might have strong consolation, who have fled for refuge to lay hold of the hope set before us. This hope we have as an anchor of the soul, both sure and steadfast, and which enters the Presence behind the veil, here the forerunner has entered for us, even Jesus, having become High Priest forever according to the order of Melchizedek.
>
> Hebrews 6:16-20

 "It is impossible for God to lie because there is no darkness, no lie, no sin in Him."

Hebrews 6:18 teaches us that "by two immutable things" we can have hope. The first is that *God is unchangeable.* He is the Rock of our Salvation and He does not change (Malachi 3:6). The second immutable thing is that *God cannot lie.* It is impossible for Him to lie because there is no darkness, no lie, no sin in Him. Therefore, Abraham determined that God could perform what He promised because God could not change, and He could not lie. Based on these two immutable, unchangeable truths, Abraham had hope in God and could endure patiently.

In Romans 4:13-25, Paul recounts the Old Testament story of how Abraham received his blessing. I will highlight some of those verses here, but I also encourage you to take a few minutes right now to read this amazing account of faith. God had promised Abraham that he would be the father of many nations—Abraham was 99 years old when God spoke this to him!

Romans 4:13 says: "For the promise that he would be the heir of the world was not to Abraham or to his seed through the law, but through the righteousness of faith." Clearly, Abraham's promise could only be fulfilled by faith, not through observance of the law. In other words, he received the promise through believing God's Word, not through doing things "right." We know that "without faith it is impossible to please Him, for he who comes to God must believe that He is, and that He is a rewarder of those who diligently seek Him" (Hebrews 11:6).

The Lord wants us to know that we can overcome unbelief and have the faith we need to see great things happen. In Matthew 17:20, Jesus said, "I say to you, if you have faith as a mustard seed, you will say to this mountain, 'Move from here to there,' and it will move; and nothing will be impossible for you." When we have faith in God, truly, nothing is impossible for us!

> As it is written, "I have made you a father of many nations" in the presence of Him whom he believed—God, who gives life to the dead and calls those things which do not exist as though they did ...
>
> Romans 4:17

Notice Paul's observations about God, which Abraham surely must have believed: God gives life to the dead (Romans 4:17). Abraham had to believe this both while he was waiting for God's promises to come to pass and surely again when God asked him to sacrifice Isaac (see Genesis 22:1-14).

We must remember that God also gives life to the things that appear "dead" or impossible in our lives. This is the message of the Cross.

God "calls those things which do not exist as though they did" (Romans 4:17). God is the Creator, and we must believe in His ability to bring things into being in our lives just as He gave Isaac, the son of promise, to an old, barren couple.

These two truths that Abraham believed cover everything: If something exists and dies, God can give life to it; and if something does not exist, He can bring it into existence because He is the Creator.

We will need to believe and apply to our lives the same truths Abraham believed and acted if we are going to appropriate all Jesus did at the Cross:

† In Hebrews 6, we saw that Abraham believed that God was unchangeable and that He could not and would not lie.

† Then in Romans 4, we learned that Abraham knew that God gives life to the dead. He is the God of the resurrection.

† And because God is the Creator, He calls things that do not exist as though they do exist.

What did Abraham do?

> Who, contrary to hope, in hope believed, so that he became the father of many nations, according to what was spoken, "So shall your descendants be." And not being weak in faith, he did not consider his own body, already dead (since he was about a hundred years old), and the deadness of Sarah's womb. He did not waver at the promise of God through unbelief, but was strengthened in faith, giving glory to God, and being fully convinced that what He had promised He was also able to perform.
>
> Romans 4:18-21

Contrary to his circumstances, in hope Abraham believed God. He did not consider the natural facts of his age or the time that had passed since God's promise. Romans 4:20 says that he did not waver at the promise of God through unbelief, but was strengthened in faith, giving glory to God.

This is very important. Abraham did not let unbelief overwhelm him. Abraham and his wife could not have children, but Abraham believed God's promise to him. Abraham would have given up if he had considered the many years of personal experience, which said that his wife's womb was old and dead and that no children would come from it. But Abraham knew the Lord was true. God's Word is true. And sure enough, His promises were fulfilled, just as He said.

Unbelief can come to us in waves when it appears that the promises from God are delayed. One of our problems, especially in these times, is that we want everything now; we have little endurance to continue in faith.

"Unbelief comes to us in waves when it appears that the promises from God are delayed"

I am not talking about having faith in faith, but faith in a person, in God Himself and in His Word.

God is able to perform what He has promised (see Romans 4:21). Abraham did not look at his circumstances and decide that God's promise was not feasible. Instead, he fixed His eyes on God and His faithfulness. That is *"the righteousness of faith"* (Romans 4:13).

Abraham did not ask to understand what God had promised; he simply received by faith. He did not consider the facts about his life, most of which made the fulfillment of God's promise seem impossible. Focusing on facts will exhaust us, which is why Romans 8:6 says,

"For to be carnally minded is death, but to be spiritually minded is life and peace."

Circumstances and facts are always subject to change, so we focus on the truth of God's Word, which never changes. This is what I call "Fact versus Truth." The facts are what we see and experience, but as I said previously, *they will change*. The truth is found in God's Word and it *never* changes. Where is your trust—in facts or in the truth?

Abraham did not set his mind on the facts of his situation but decided instead to focus on God and to declare His glory. Abraham was strengthened in faith as He set his heart on the Lord and worshiped Him. When we praise God and declare His faithfulness, our faith will be strengthened too. What if God does not answer our prayers, how long do we continue? We never stop; we continue to praise and worship God, giving glory to Him.

> Now it was not written for his sake alone that it was imputed to him, but also for us. It shall be imputed to us who believe in Him who raised up Jesus our Lord from the dead, who was delivered up because of our offenses, and was raised because of our justification.
>
> Romans 4:23-25

Remember the passage in Romans 8:6? There is a principle in the Kingdom of God that indicates whatever we set our minds on will direct our lives. The mind set on the flesh is death and the mind set on the Spirit will be life and peace.

The same holds true about whatever we focus on. If we focus on God, we will become like Him. If we focus on our problems and circumstances, they will seem to get bigger and bigger.

> Now the Lord is the Spirit; and where the Spirit of the Lord is, there is liberty. But we all, with unveiled face, beholding

as in a mirror the glory of the Lord, are being transformed into the same image from glory to glory, just as by the Spirit of the Lord.

2 Corinthians 3:17- 18

We are transformed into God's image as we behold Him. I can confidently say, if we are not beholding Him but are beholding our circumstances, they will overwhelm us.

> "We are transformed into God's image as we behold Him."

You may be asking, "How are we to behold Him?" Hebrews 12:1 tells us:

> Therefore we also, since we are surrounded by so great a cloud of witnesses, let us lay aside every weight, and the sin which so easily ensnares us, and let us run with endurance the race that is set before us, looking unto Jesus, the author and finisher of our faith, who for the joy that was set before Him endured the Cross, despising the shame, and has sat down at the right hand of the throne of God.

We are told to lay aside the sin that so easily ensnares us—not "sins," but "the sin." I believe "the sin" is unbelief. Unbelief is indeed sin; it keeps us from the promises of God and from having faith in God's ability to perform what He has promised. Unbelief comes from focusing on our problems and the circumstances that are often contrary to God's promises. The more we focus on these negative things, the more unbelief increases. How can we lay aside the sin of unbelief? We do this by asking for forgiveness for our unbelief and repenting of it, because it is sin.

Then, we look unto Jesus, the author and finisher of our faith. Faith begins and ends in Jesus. The word *look* means we are to look away from something and turn and give focus to something else. Obviously, we must turn away from the negative circumstances we face (where unbelief comes from) and start looking to Jesus.

We look unto Jesus by spending time in the Word and focusing on Him instead of focusing on our problems. You can start focusing on Him by reviewing the exchange of the Cross and committing to memorize all the benefits of this exchange.

Psalms 103:1-5 tells us to stir up our souls, to bless the Lord and not to forget all of His benefits. Through praise and worship, we can look unto Jesus, giving Him glory, by praising and thanking Him for all He has done.

Abide in the Word

Unless we abide in the Word, we will not know what we have inherited. We must spend time in the Word so we will know what God has given us through the Cross. God has recorded His entire will and testament in the Bible, and in order to know what our inheritance is, we must read and study His Word. Jesus said in John 8:31: "If you abide in My word, you are My disciples indeed."

We must also remember that faith comes from hearing the Word (see Romans 10:17). We cannot abide in the Word unless we first hear it.

We "hear" the Word of God as we (a) read it for ourselves and meditate on it or (b) hear others read it. Joshua 1:8 says: "This Book of the Law shall not depart from your mouth, but you shall *meditate* in it day and night, that you may observe to do according to all that is written in it. For then you will make your way prosperous, and then you will have good success" (emphasis mine). In this verse, the word, *meditate* means, "to mutter." In the biblical sense, to meditate would be similar to what a cow does as it chews its cud, ruminating the same food over and over and over and over. We meditate on the Word, keep confessing it, and speak it over and over again—not to get something from God but because it is truth, and truth makes us free (see John 8:32).

SUMMARY

† We receive the work of the Cross in our lives by faith and only by faith. We cannot earn it or pay for it.

† Receiving any inheritance is based on believing a promise, and God's Word is His promise. We can trust Him to fulfill His promise to us. While we have faith, we must exhibit patience until we see the promises fulfilled.

† God is unchangeable and He cannot lie—so we know that we can have hope in God's promises and endure patiently until the day we see those promises come to pass.

† God has resurrection power!

† We must repent for the sin of unbelief and start looking unto Jesus who is the author and finisher of our faith.

† Circumstances and facts may change, but we must focus on the truth of God's Word and the truth of His nature.

† God has power we don't fully understand. If something exists and dies, God can give life to it. If something does not exist, God can bring it into existence because He is the Creator!

† We must abide in the Word and remember that faith comes from hearing the Word. We need to set our minds on God and His Word. We are to praise and worship the Lord, giving glory to Him.

♥ TAKE IT TO HEART

The book of Hebrews (11:1) tells us that, "Faith is the substance of things hoped for, the evidence of things not seen." And that, "without faith it is impossible to please Him ..." (Heb. 11:6). This presents a challenge for most of us. How do we embrace faith? How do we step into that strength of trusting God for life's circumstances when we see so many situations that just don't seem to line up with His promises? How do we wrestle with our unbelief and find truth?

The answer is in a relationship with God, the Father. It's about abiding in His Word and knowing who He really is—Father, Son, and Holy Spirit. He longs to reveal His heart and His nature to each one of us that we might be fully enveloped in His love. Take a moment to pray and invite that revelation of truth into your life and heart.

TAKE IT TO GOD

Dear God,

I thank You that Your Word is a "lamp unto my feet and a light unto my path" to guide and show me the way of truth. I need more faith, more understanding, and a deeper place of abiding in Your Word. My unbelief has caused pain and brokenness in my life. Please forgive me and draw me nearer to You. Increase my faith. Help me to set my mind on things above, to trust You, to walk by the Spirit and to listen to Your voice as I focus on meditating in Your Word and choosing to believe in Your goodness over my life.

PART 4

The Cross Defeated the Enemy

"Jesus's accomplishment
on the Cross was a
complete and total
victory, a work that is
finished forever."

After the Cross,
the Resurrection

Why do you seek the living among the dead? He is not here, but is risen!

Luke 24:5-6

Throughout this book, we have examined primarily what Jesus accomplished through His death on the Cross. We have also looked at the benefits available to us because of Jesus's work on the Cross. But after Jesus died for us, another powerful, unprecedented event took place: His resurrection.

Many people were crucified before and during the time of Christ because crucifixion was a common form of capital punishment in those days. But no one had ever been crucified and then raised from the dead to live eternally until this happened to Jesus Christ. People were astounded!

In Acts 2:22-24, Peter preached boldly:

Men of Israel, hear these words: Jesus of Nazareth, a Man attested by God to you by miracles, wonders, and signs which God did through Him in your midst, as you your-selves also know—Him, being delivered by the determined purpose and foreknowledge of God, you have taken by lawless hands, have crucified, and put to death; whom God raised up, having loosed the pains of death, because it was not possible that He should be held by it.

> *"Jesus's resurrection is what separates Him from every other "deity", along with the historical accounts of His appearance."*

This kind of preaching about the resurrection brought persecution to the first-century Church. Paul and Jesus's disciples were persecuted because they kept talking about Christ's resurrection. Their constant references to His life after death were bothersome to the leaders of that day (see; 4:2; 10:38-43). Many religious leaders throughout history and even now argue that there are many ways to God; but it is clear that Jesus, the crucified and **resurrected** Lord, is *the* path to God. His resurrection is what separates Him from every other "deity", along with the historical accounts of His appearance.

Acts 13:28-30 says:

> And though they found no cause for death in Him, they asked Pilate that He should be put to death. Now when they had fulfilled all that was written concerning Him, they took Him down from the tree and laid Him in a tomb. But God raised Him from the dead.

According to Acts 13:28-30, God Himself raised Jesus from the dead (see also Acts 17:3, 18, 31). His resurrection secured forever and guaranteed forever the victory that Jesus paid for on the Cross. This is why the resurrection is so important for us to understand.

In Jesus's day, deceased bodies were not buried as they are today; they were placed in tombs cut out of rock. Cylindrical-type rocks were then rolled over the openings of the tombs and set into troughs so the rocks fit tightly into the openings and held them closed securely. The stones that closed the tombs were so large they could only be moved by the efforts of several strong men.

Luke 24 tells the story of what happened the morning after Jesus's burial. Because His body could not be prepared adequately for burial before the Sabbath began (by Jewish law), several women went to the tomb the next morning to perform the traditional burial preparations. When they arrived, the heavy stone covering the tomb's entrance was rolled away and Jesus's body was not inside.

Luke 24:1-7 recounts the events of that day:

> Now on the first day of the week, very early in the morning, they, and certain other women with them, came to the tomb bringing the spices which they had prepared. But they found the stone rolled away from the tomb. Then they went in and did not find the body of the Lord Jesus. And it happened, as they were greatly perplexed about this, that behold, two men stood by them in shining garments. Then, as they were afraid and bowed their faces to the earth, they said to them, "Why do you seek the living among the dead? He is not here, but is risen! Remember how He spoke to you when He was still in Galilee, saying, 'The Son of Man must be delivered into the hands of sinful men, and be crucified, and the third day rise again.'"

Notice that the women were greeted with these words, "Why do you seek the living among the dead? He is not here, but He is risen!" That statement is as wonderful for us today as it was for those women centuries ago. Jesus is not dead! He is risen to live forever.

Can you imagine what Mary and the others who went to the tomb on that early Sunday morning must have thought? I am sure their minds were racing with questions, such as: *What does this mean? Where is He? Where has He gone?*

It must have taken some time for the reality to sink in that Jesus had actually been raised from the dead. Of course, it wasn't long before Jesus began to reveal Himself to His faithful followers. Even though He had told them He would be crucified and then raised on the third day, they did not have any point of reference to help them understand what would actually take place.

Previously, Jesus had told His disciples clearly that He was going to Jerusalem to be crucified. Matthew 16:21 says, "From that time Jesus began to show to His disciples that He must go to Jerusalem and suffer many things from the elders and chief priests and scribes, and be killed, and be raised the third day." And in Matthew 17:22-23, we read that "Now while they were staying in Galilee, Jesus said to them, "The Son of Man is about to be betrayed into the hands of men, and they will kill Him, and the third day He will be raised up." I encourage you also to read Matthew 20:17-19.

Though Jesus had demonstrated His power to raise the dead with Lazarus, they still struggled to really believe in His resurrection. This was understandably difficult because they had seen the pain and suffering He endured, watched His dead body being removed from the Cross, and witnessed the sealing of His body in a tomb. They were perplexed when they saw Him again after the resurrection.

Jesus's Power over Death

The story of Lazarus in John 11 is a beautiful example of Jesus's power over death. Jesus's friend Lazarus became sick. When Lazarus' sisters called for Jesus to come, He told His disciples that He would go in a few days because Lazarus' sickness was not unto death, but for the glory of God (see John 11:4). Then later, Jesus told His disciples that He must go to Lazarus because he was "sleeping", and He needed to wake him (see John 11:11). His disciples stated that if Lazarus "slept," then he would get well. Jesus then clarified to them that Lazarus was not sleeping as human beings sleep, but that he was dead.

Isn't it interesting that Jesus refers to death as sleep? One reason for this is that the reality for those who believe in Christ is that death is simply a transition from this life to the next. We tend to see it as terminal, but Jesus does not see it that way.

When Jesus goes to find Lazarus, Lazarus' sister Martha confronts Him, saying that had He been there sooner, Lazarus would not have died. She answered Him that she understood Lazarus would rise again in the resurrection at the last day (perhaps indicating that her family were Pharisees, because Pharisees believed in a resurrection at the "last day"). He responds in John 11:25- 26: "Jesus said to her, 'I am the resurrection and the life. He who believes in Me, though he may die, he shall live. And whoever lives and believes in Me shall never die. Do you believe this?'"

Jesus says that He *is* the resurrection and the life. What a powerful statement! Even before Jesus went to the Cross and paid for our sins with His life, He had the power to raise the dead and give life to all who believe in Him—life now and life forever.

As mentioned before, the resurrection secures forever what Jesus paid for at the Cross. It also gives us hope because it reminds us that life comes from death. This hope is a key to our faith. Since everything comes by faith, it is imperative for our hope to be strong.

Abraham believed that God gives life to the dead. Paul writes about this in Romans 4:17-18: "(as it is written, 'I have made you a father of many nations') in the presence of Him whom he believed—God, who gives life to the dead and calls those things which do not exist as though they did; who, contrary to hope, in hope believed"

"Our belief in God who brings life to dead places is our source of hope."

Believing that God gives life to the dead and believing in the resurrection is foundational if we are going to have hope. In fact, our belief in God as one who gives life to the dead is the source of our hope. Even if our dreams and expectations seem dead (and in some cases *are* dead), because of the power of the resurrection and the promise of eternal life, God can give life to our dead dreams. Whatever existed, even though it appears dead, can live.

In addition to giving life to the dead, according to Romans 4:17-18, God calls things that do not exist as though they did. Since He is the Creator, nothing is impossible. If something existed and died, He can give life to it. If it doesn't exist, He can create it. This is the reason Abraham had hope, completely contrary to his circumstances.

The reason we can believe just as Abraham believed is explained in Colossians 1:15-18:

> He is the image of the invisible God, the firstborn over all creation. For by Him all things were created that are in heaven and that are on earth, visible and invisible, whether thrones or dominions or principalities or powers. All things were created through Him and for Him. And He is before all things, and in Him all things consist. And He is the head of the body, the church, who is the beginning, the firstborn from the dead, that in all things He may have the preeminence.

Jesus is the firstborn from the dead and all things were created through Him and for Him. In Him, all things consist.

The Anchor of Our Faith

Paul was serious about preaching the resurrection to the people he encountered. Read the following account from 1 Corinthians 15:3-8:

> For I delivered to you first of all that which I also received: that Christ died for our sins according to the Scriptures, and that He was buried, and that He rose again the third day according to the Scriptures, and that He was seen by Cephas, then by the twelve. After that He was seen by over five hundred brethren at once, of whom the greater part remain to the present, but some have fallen asleep. After that He was seen by James, then by all the apostles. Then last of all He was seen by me also, as by one born out of due time.

Paul continues in this passage to explain the futility of believing the Gospel if the resurrection itself is not true:

> Now if Christ is preached that He has been raised from the dead, how do some among you say that there is no resurrection of the dead? But if there is no resurrection of the dead, then Christ is not risen. And if Christ is not risen, then our preaching is empty and your faith is also empty. Yes, and we are found false witnesses of God, because we have testified of God that He raised up Christ, whom He did not raise up—if in fact the dead do not rise. For if the dead do not rise, then Christ is not risen. And if Christ is not risen, your faith is futile; you are still in your sins!
>
> 1 Corinthians 15:13-17

Paul didn't see the resurrection as a secondary issue; he saw it as extremely important, the lynchpin or anchor of our faith. If Jesus wasn't raised from the dead, then we have some problems with what we believe. But He *was* raised from the dead—and we have solutions!

In Romans 8:11, we discover the source of the power of the resurrection and how it affects us: "But if the Spirit of Him who raised Jesus from the dead dwells in you, He who raised Christ from the dead will also give life to your mortal bodies through His Spirit who dwells in you."

It is the Holy Spirit who raised Jesus from the dead and it is the same Holy Spirit who gives life to our own mortal bodies.

The fact that the Holy Spirit raised Jesus from the dead and gives life to us is "the exceeding greatness of His power toward us who believe," mentioned in Ephesians 1:19-21:

> ...and what is the exceeding greatness of His power toward us who believe, according to the working of His mighty power which He worked in Christ when He raised Him from the dead and seated Him at His right hand in the heavenly places, far above all principality and power and might and dominion, and every name that is named, not only in this age but also in that which is to come.

It's not our own power; it's *His* power! This exceeding great power, if we believe, is the same power that was exerted to raise Jesus from the dead. It is the Holy Spirit that raised Him, and it is the Holy Spirit who is available to you and me.

"It is vital that we realize the power of the resurrection, relying on the power of the Holy Spirit to bring breakthrough."

Many times, I talk with people who say they just can't overcome or break through problems in their lives. Sometimes they indicate they just don't know how to do it. We need to know the truth about how powerful the resurrection is, and we must believe that resurrection power is available to us. It is vital that we realize the power of the resurrection and rely on that power of the Holy Spirit to bring the breakthrough we need.

> Yet indeed I also count all things loss for the excellence of the knowledge of Christ Jesus my Lord, for whom I have suffered the loss of all things, and count them as rubbish, that I may gain Christ and be found in Him, not having my own righteousness, which is from the law, but that which is through faith in Christ, the righteousness which is from God by faith, that I may know Him and the power of His resurrection...
>
> Philippians 3:8-10

In Philippians 3:4-7, the verses preceding the passage above, Paul gives an account of his upbringing, which was extremely respectable to the religious people of his day. His lineage and education were outstanding, but he valued something else even more. He writes in Philippians 3:8 that he considered all of those things as loss so he could "gain Christ." He knew his righteousness was not rooted in doing things the right way, but in knowing Christ and the power of His resurrection. When Paul saw what was happening in the Kingdom of God around him, he realized that the resurrection was the only source of power. Everything else, without Christ, was trash to him.

At the point when Paul wrote his letter to the Philippians, even though he had seen the dead raised, people healed, demons cast out, and preached the Gospel to many parts of the known world, he still wanted to see more. He knew he had not attained all of what he wanted. He refused to give up his desire for everything God had for him.

Press On

Through the Cross, each one of us is a new creation. Our pasts are cut off; everything in our pasts is completely remitted or cancelled. As believers, we can't drag the past into the present with us. If we worry about the past, the enemy will use it to hold us back. We must forget what's behind us, let Christ's blood cover it, and let His resurrection return to life what was dead. If we allow yesterday to hold us captive, it will steal today. We can't change what happened yesterday, but we can choose life today. We can live today by the presence of God and the power of the resurrection. We have no guarantee for tomorrow, and we can't change yesterday. Today is all we have.

On the Cross, Christ was crucified between two thieves. I call them, the "thief of yesterday" and the "thief of tomorrow." We cannot let the past steal our present from us; and, we cannot let the fear of the future steal from us either.

Paul writes in Philippians 3:14: "I press toward the goal for the prize of the upward call of God in Christ Jesus." Just as Paul did, we need to press toward the goal, "for the prize of the upward call of God in Christ Jesus."

Understanding the resurrection and its power is essential to our walk and our ability to "press on." *The resurrection secures and guarantees forever what Jesus paid for at the Cross.* This power is available for you and me to walk in daily. This is why the resurrection is so critical for us to understand.

SUMMARY

† Even though Jesus's resurrection was foretold, His friends and the people of His day still did not expect it and found it difficult to believe.

† Death is simply a transition from this earthly life to the eternal life that awaits us. This is why Christ referred to Lazarus' death of Lazarus as "sleep."

† Christ *is* the resurrection and the life.

† The resurrection is the source of our hope. If we can trust in the resurrection, we have the hope and the faith to believe for anything God says, contrary to our circumstances perhaps, but completely in alignment with God's promises.

† With God, nothing is impossible. If you have dreams or expectations that seem dead, God can breathe life into them.

† The Holy Spirit, who is the power of the resurrection, is available to you too! The same power that raised Christ from the dead still brings breakthrough today.

† Today is all you have. Don't let your past direct your life today; and don't worry or fret about tomorrow. Live today and be filled with Jesus's resurrection power!

The Complete Victory
of the Cross

Jesus came to earth and lived and died so we could be free—free from the power and fear of death, free from sin, free from sickness, free from every kind of bondage that could ever ensnare us. The Cross represents the greatest victory of all time. Jesus's accomplishment on the Cross was a complete and total victory, a work that is finished forever. He did this work for us so that we could be free and experience the fullness of His presence and advance His Kingdom on earth. In this chapter, we will look at Jesus's total victory, the truth that He completely defeated the devil and set us free so that we can live in His victory—all because of the Cross.

Up to this point, we have hardly mentioned the devil. The devil is real, and we must be on the alert for him, but knowing about him is secondary to knowing the truth. I sometimes hear people say they are always "fighting the devil." This is an out-of-balance situation. If we will grow in and appropriate the truth of God's Word into our lives by faith, we will not "fight the devil" all the time. He is defeated and we have the victory over him because of the victory Jesus won for us.

There was a time in my life when I thought God and the devil were fighting it out to see who would win. I just hoped that God would win. When I discovered the truth, I realized that God had already defeated the devil. This means you and I have victory over him also because of the victory that Jesus won for us at the Cross.

Some of the Apostle John's writings reveal how important Jesus's victory is. Please read John 12:27-33. In this passage, Jesus told His disciples what was about to happen. He said, "Now the ruler of this world will be cast out" (John 12:31). In other words, Jesus told His disciples *before* He went to the Cross that He would defeat the devil.

In 1 John 3:8, John is much older and writing as a father in the Lord. Reflecting on why Jesus came and what Jesus did, he writes: "He who sins is of the devil, for the devil has sinned from the beginning. For this purpose the Son of God was manifested, that He might destroy the works of the devil" (1 John 3:8).

Notice the passage below. This was recorded *after* the Cross and before the coming of the Holy Spirit who would bring conviction and reveal the full victory of the Cross to people's hearts. Jesus declares that, "the ruler of this world is judged." It is a finished work. The enemy has been judged; the Son of God has defeated him forever.

> And when He has come, He will convict the world of sin, and of righteousness, and of judgment: of sin, because they do not believe in Me; of righteousness, because I go to My Father and you see Me no more; of judgment, because the ruler of this world is judged.
>
> John 16:8-11

Jesus was indicating to His disciples that it was good for Him to go away so the Holy Spirit could come. The Holy Spirit would convict the world of sin, righteousness and judgment, because the ruler of the world (Satan) is judged. Jesus was saying that all of this would happen *after* the Cross.

Our Present Enemy

We need to know that we have a real enemy who is bent on our destruction—to steal, to kill and to destroy (see John 10:10). Realizing the fact that there is a spiritual battle raging and that I do have an enemy made Scripture come alive to me years ago. When God changed my life in 1982, words began to jump off the page at me related to "your adversary, the devil" (1 Peter 5:8).

Before I attended the conference that changed my life in 1982, I had no idea a battle was raging in the spiritual realm. I didn't know anything about the devil and had never thought about demons or what they did. I hadn't even considered the fact Scripture tells us Jesus cast out demons. I didn't know what happened in the book of Acts or whether it applied to me today. When I was filled with the Holy Spirit in that meeting, I began to understand there was a spiritual war and Jesus had already won the victory in it.

"Our nature is to avoid war (conflict), but the reality is that we are engaged in spiritual warfare whether we like it or not."

Before I even knew there was a battle, I was already in bondage, a "prisoner of war," so to speak. Our nature is to avoid war, but the reality is that we are engaged in spiritual warfare whether we like it or not (see Ephesians 6:12). We are God's representatives, sent to possess the land. There is land we are to possess, but it is not vacant. The devil doesn't want to give up what he already has; but we are in the midst of this war and are charged to take back the ground the enemy has taken.

The Apostle Paul also writes in Colossians 2:15 of Jesus's absolute triumph over the devil and all of the demonic hosts. He knew that, in those days, Roman soldiers paraded their battle spoils through the streets in a grand display that exhibited the annihilation of their enemies. This is exactly what Jesus did at the Cross; He totally annihilated principalities and powers. Colossians 2:15 says: "Having disarmed principalities and powers, He made a public spectacle of them, triumphing over them in it."

Colossians 1:13 says: "He has delivered us from the power of darkness and conveyed us into the Kingdom of the Son of His love." Notice that this verse is written in the past tense. The work is finished. When we are in Christ, we are delivered from the power of darkness and translated into the Kingdom of God's Son. We are no longer trying to escape the power of darkness or be translated into His Kingdom. He has already done those things for us and rescued us from the ruler of this world. This is a present reality in our lives as believers. Jesus won the victory for us. We cannot do one thing to earn or to pay for this triumph. We simply receive it by faith, as His gift.

We have been taken out of the enemy's authority structure and brought into the Kingdom. We are each a new creation and have been made righteous. The devil may try to lie to us, saying that we cannot be free, but we don't have to believe that. Remember: Colossians 1:13 is in the past tense. Jesus has already done for us what is promised in that verse.

"Jesus's triumph over the enemy is as real today as it was 2,000 years ago."

The verse below affirms that Jesus won an absolute, total victory: "I am He who lives, and was dead, and behold, I am alive forevermore. Amen. And I have the keys of Hades and of Death" (Revelation 1:18). His triumph over the enemy is as real today as it was 2000 years ago.

Throughout Scripture, Jesus makes very clear who He is. Because Jesus has won the victory for us, we can live on earth as representatives of the King of kings and Lord of lords. It is time for us to appropriate this victory by faith. It is time for us to look like Jesus, act like Jesus, evict the enemy from every area of our lives and advance the Kingdom of God on earth. Who has the keys of Hades and of Death? Not the devil, because Jesus has the keys!

Jesus's Victory, Our Victory

If you have been in church very long, you have probably heard a sermon on Matthew 28:18-20, with the emphasis on going into all nations. This is a very popular passage for missions conferences and evangelistic outreaches.

> And Jesus came and spoke to them, saying, "All authority has been given to Me in heaven and on earth. Go therefore and make disciples of all the nations, baptizing them in the name of the Father and of the Son and of the Holy Spirit, teaching them to observe all things that I have commanded you; and lo, I am with you always, even to the end of the age." Amen.
>
> Matthew 28:18-20

One day when I was meditating on this passage, the Lord spoke to me and said I was missing the most important parts of this passage. I believe the reason we are able to make disciples of all people groups is found in the phrases just before and after the command to "go." In verse 18, He says He has all authority on Heaven and on earth. It is because of this authority that we can go and make disciples. I also believe that, in verse 20, the key to going and making disciples of all nations is, "I will be with you always."

Man lost his authority to rule when he sinned in the Garden. Jesus always had authority in Heaven; it was man's delegated authority that was lost in the fall, which Jesus purchased with His life so we could again rule and reign on earth "in Christ."

Matthew 28 declares that Jesus has all authority in Heaven and on earth. For this reason, He sends us to go and make disciples, to baptize and to teach them. He knows we can accomplish these tasks because of the authority He gives us. Jesus purchased all authority on the Cross and when we are in Him, we can walk in the same authority He has. As believers, we identify completely with Him and His authority is ours.

In addition to Jesus having all authority in Heaven and earth, He promises us in verse 20 that He would never leave us but would be with us to the end. This should be all we need.

Because we have the authority of Jesus, we do not need to be constantly defeated by the enemy. We may be harassed, but we don't have to live in defeat. About one-third of Jesus's recorded ministry dealt with casting out demons or pushing back the enemy. He expects us to exercise that same authority as a normal, everyday part of our active, maturing spiritual lives. As we see in the following verses, casting out demons is a part of our lives, but is not nearly as important as the fact our names are written in Heaven—that we belong to Jesus and share in His life.

> Then the seventy returned with joy, saying, "Lord, even the demons are subject to us in Your name." And He said to them, "I saw Satan fall like lightening from heaven. Behold, I give you the authority to trample on serpents and scorpions, and over all the power of the enemy, and nothing shall by any means hurt you. Nevertheless do not rejoice in this, that the spirits are subject to you, but rather rejoice because your names are written in heaven."
>
> Luke 10:17-20

What a great passage. God didn't only use the twelve disciples to minister; He used people just like you and me, according to Luke 10:17-20. They were so excited when they discovered the demons had to obey when they used His name. Jesus made it very clear that Satan was defeated, and He had given them authority to rule over serpents and scorpions and over all the power of the enemy.

Two important words we need to examine are used in this passage. The first word is *authority*. The Greek word translated *authority* in English is *exousia*. The Vine's Dictionary defines *exousia* as, "it is lawful, or it is right to exercise power." Jesus's authority gives us the right to cast out demons and have authority over the devil. Jesus has all authority and because we are "in Him," we can operate in His authority.

The enemy does not have authority over you and me unless we give authority to him through sin. When we sin, we give him authority in our lives and he comes to steal, kill and destroy us (see John 10:10).

Though the devil does not have authority, he does have power. *Power* is the second word we need to understand. In Luke 10:19, Jesus said He has given us authority over the devil's power, and nothing shall hurt us. The Greek word translated *power* is *dunamis*, which *Vine's Dictionary* defines as, "force or ability, power of action". We receive power—the miraculous power of God—from the Holy Spirit when He comes upon us.

"We receive the power of God from the Holy Spirit, when He comes upon us."

"In Christ," we have authority and by the Holy Spirit, we have power. The truth is, the authority is His and the power is from the Holy Spirit, but we get to operate in both when we are sons and daughters of God, walking in fellowship with Him.

> Then I heard a loud voice saying in heaven, "Now salvation, and strength, and the Kingdom of our God, and the power of His Christ have come, for the accuser of our brethren,

who accused them before our God day and night, has been cast down. And they overcame him by the blood of the Lamb and by the word of their testimony, and they did not love their lives to the death.

Revelation 12:10-11

All of us are to walk in the truth that, "salvation, strength, the Kingdom of our God and the power of His Christ have come." Yes, salvation *has* come. We need to appropriate that salvation (which literally means, "to save, to be delivered, and to be healed") into our lives. Also, God's strength has come. *Strength* comes from the Greek word *dunamis,* which could be translated *power.* This power is from the Holy Spirit. In addition, the Kingdom of God has come. This means that the rule and reign of King Jesus is now in effect. He has always ruled in Heaven; now His rule has come on earth. When Jesus began His earthly ministry, He both declared and demonstrated the Kingdom of God and by exercising His authority and power over sin, sickness, and the devil. The power of Christ has also come. This word, *power,* comes from the Greek word *exousia,* which means Christ's authority.

As you can see from Revelation 12:10-11, everything we need has come down from Heaven and been given to us so we can live victoriously: salvation, the Holy Spirit (who is the power of God), the Kingdom's rule and reign, and Christ's full authority to accomplish His work on earth.

There is no problem—no war—in Heaven. When Satan was kicked out of Heaven, he fell like lightning to earth (see Luke 10:18), so he no longer operates there. The problem is on earth; we fight the spiritual battle in the earthly realm. Now is the time for us to join Jesus in His victory and in His work of bringing His complete rule and reign from Heaven to earth. What a privilege! We join Jesus in His victory and overcome the devil.

The Blood of the Lamb...

Revelation 12:11 says we overcome the devil by the blood of the Lamb. This encompasses everything in this book thus far. The blood of the Lamb is Jesus's blood shed at the Cross. God's Word tells us we are sanctified by the blood;

"Our personal stories and experiences are powerful weapons in our hands."

we have forgiveness of sin by the blood; we have peace through the blood; we are washed and cleansed by the blood; and now we overcome by the blood. Jesus shed His blood for us, in the following ways:

† He prayed so intensely that He shed blood in Gethsemane

† He was struck in the face and bled.

† He bled from His head as a result of the punctures from the crown of thorns.

† He was beaten on His back until blood poured forth from His body.

† He bled where the nails pierced His hands and feet.

† He was pierced in the side by a spear where blood and water poured out.

The shedding of Jesus's blood is the reason we can overcome anything that opposes us. It is all about what Jesus did at the Cross. His victory is our victory.

The Word of Our Testimony...

Revelation 12:11 also tells us we overcome by "the word of our testimony." There are at least two factors I believe are important to consider concerning the word of our testimony. First, the personal testimony of how Jesus saved us and revealed Himself to us is a mighty weapon. We overcome by the word of our testimony. The devil cannot take our personal experiences and stories from us, and they are powerful weapons in our hands. We need to tell people what Jesus did for us.

As we consider the "word of our testimony," we need to think about the Word itself—the Word of God. The Word is the sword of the Spirit and it is a weapon (Ephesians 6:17). Jesus used the Word against the devil in the wilderness. He said, "It is written, that man shall not live by bread alone but by every word that proceeds from the mouth of God." (Matthew 4:4). If Jesus used the Word, the sword of the Spirit, as an offensive weapon, we must also.

Loving Not Our Lives...

Revelation 12:11 also specifies that another way we overcome is to "love not our lives unto death." If we are going to appropriate all that He paid for at the Cross and live in His victory, then we really need to be wholeheartedly committed, "sold out" to Jesus. We must not be lovers of ourselves, but whole-hearted lovers of God, willingly laying our lives down for Him.

The Challenge of Walking in Victory

In 1 John 2:14, the Apostle John talks about defeating the enemy. He writes: "I have written to you, fathers, because you have known Him who is from the beginning. I have written to you, young men, because you are strong, and the word of God abides in you, and you have overcome the wicked one."

God has given us incredible authority in the power of His Word. We exercise our authority as we abide in the Word and use it to overcome the wicked one. We must rise up and resist the enemy.

It's important that we maintain our physical health and building strong muscles and stamina is important for a long life. Some people use weights for their workout routine to help build stronger bones and muscles. There is an aspect of building up our spiritual muscles that often gets overlooked. We see in the Scriptures that the Lord allows the enemy to be our spiritual antagonist (so to speak) so we will build resistance and grow strong in God and be strengthened in our faith. God often uses the enemy as our "trainer" in the workout room of the spirit. While it's true that the victory is sealed for us; however, we do have to utilize that strength and engage with the enemy. We shouldn't be battling the devil all the time, but we need to use the spiritual muscles that God gave us!

> *"God often uses the enemy as our "trainer" in the workout room of the spirit."*

Even though Jesus Christ won a complete and final victory for us at the Cross, the enemy still attacks us. The fact that Jesus has already won does not mean the devil will leave us alone. Remember that 1 John 3:8 says, "For this purpose the Son of God was manifested, that He might destroy the works of the devil." Jesus broke the stronghold of the enemy's authority and destroyed the *works* of the devil but did not destroy the devil himself. We still have an enemy, as 1 Peter 5:8 reminds us: "Be sober, be vigilant; because your adversary the devil walks about like a roaring lion, seeking whom he may devour."

We are at war and the devil will lie and deceive us in every way he can. In fact, the primary weapons he has are lies and deceit. Two of the lies he often speaks are: "I am not defeated. I have more power than God," and "You have no authority. You have to stay in bondage."

You may remember movies you have seen over the past 20-25 years. Many of them depict the devil as absolutely the worst, the biggest, and the most evil being who ever existed. Other movies show him as a fairytale character, a joke, something that no one would actually believe in. But both of those are lies. The enemy wants to portray himself in one of those two ways so that we don't even bother messing with him. The devil is real.

We have victory over the enemy because Jesus won it for us, but we must fight *in the power of the Lord*, not in our own strength. Our authority and our strength are in Him. We must be aggressive in our faith and in appropriating everything Jesus did for us. Paul urges us toward the end of his letter to the Ephesians: "Finally, my brethren, be strong in the Lord and in the power of His might" (Ephesians 6:10).

The enemy attacks us primarily in our minds. One way we can actively resist him is to guard our thoughts diligently. The enemy knows that Romans 8:6 is true, so he is always working to get us to focus on earthly things, circumstances or problems in order to work death in us. The mind set on the Spirit is life and peace. This is the battle. When we take thoughts captive (see 2 Corinthians 10:4) and focus on the things of the Spirit, we defeat the enemy.

> For to be carnally minded is death, but to be spiritually minded is life and peace.
>
> Romans 8:6

God knew the enemy would resist us and try to talk us out of believing everything Jesus did for us. As we walk in the victory of the Cross, we must appropriate the "exceeding greatness of His power toward us who believe, according to the working of His mighty power which he worked in Christ when He raised Him from the dead and seated Him at His right hand in the heavenly places, far above all principality and power and might and dominion, and every name that is named ..." (Ephesians 1:19-21). Let's re-examine this passage because it's so essential to our beliefs.

The *exceeding greatness of God's power* is toward us if we believe. This is the same power that raised Jesus from the dead and seated Him far above everything. It is the Holy Spirit who raised Jesus from the dead and it is the Holy Spirit who gives us this power.

"God often uses the enemy as our "trainer" in the workout room of the spirit."

Exceeding great power is available to us and for us to overcome the enemy.

Jesus is also able to do far more than we could ever ask or think, "according to the power that works in us" (Ephesians 3:20). This is the power of the Holy Spirit.

God has given us everything so we can live victoriously and overcome in this life. The devil does not want us to know he is defeated, that we have authority over him and all his forces, and that the power of God, the Holy Spirit, lives in us.

Acts 1:8 says, "But you shall receive power when the Holy Spirit has come upon you; and you shall be witnesses to Me in Jerusalem, and in all Judea and Samaria, and to the ends of the earth." Jesus has given the Holy Spirit to live in us and empower us to live victoriously. We must be baptized with the Holy Spirit if we are going to live in victory.

Securing the Victory

> Therefore submit to God. Resist the devil and he will flee
> from you.
>
> James 4:7

To walk in victory, the first thing we must do is to submit to God.
We need to submit to Him before we resist the devil. Sometimes
we get this backwards: we resist God and submit to the devil. But
we need to do this in the proper order; we can only resist the devil
effectively and see him flee according to God's promise if we *first*
submit to God.

Know the truth of the Word and believe that:

† God loves you and you are His child.

† the Cross is the power of God.

† the victory of the Cross belongs to you through Jesus Christ.

Do you realize there are songs being sung around the Throne in
Heaven to the King of Kings? Songs declaring His majesty, His omnipo-
tence, His love, and His sacrifice for all mankind.

> And they sang a new song, saying: "You are worthy to take
> the scroll, and to open its seals; for You were slain, and have
> redeemed us to God by Your blood out of every tribe and
> tongue and people and nation, and have made us kings and
> priests to our God; and we shall reign on the earth."
>
> Revelation 5:9-10

When Jesus taught His disciples to pray, He said to pray that earth
would look like

Heaven—that what's happening there would happen here! On earth as it is in Heaven (Matthew 6:10). Freedom comes when we lift our eyes unto Him who sits on the throne.

This song from Revelation 5:9-10 is being sung in Heaven and declarations are being made 24/7 that the Lamb who was slain would win from every people group on the face of this earth those who would long to be free and brought into His Kingdom.

God's plan from the beginning was to redeem mankind to rule and reign on earth and walk in the authority purchased for us on the Cross. So we join with all of Heaven in singing this New Song – "Holy, holy, holy, Lord God Almighty, Who was and is and is to come!" (Revelation 4:8)

In closing out this chapter, allow me to present some questions for you to consider as you wrestle for faith, to believe the truth of God's Word, His love for you, and the power of the Cross.

† What does Jesus's victory mean to you personally?

† What was Jesus's purpose in coming to earth, according to 1 John 3:8?

† Are there any "works of the devil" operating in your life? What are they, and how can they be destroyed?

† Are you guarding your thoughts diligently? What Scriptures can you use that will help you?

† How do you walk in Jesus's victory?

SUMMARY

† Jesus came to win. He intended to defeat the devil; and He did.

† Jesus won the victory for us. Nothing we could have done would have "helped" Jesus win. We certainly couldn't earn, pay for it, or win the victory ourselves. We must receive it by faith as His gift to us.

† Jesus's victory is our victory. Because of Christ's victory, we have authority in Him. We can walk in the same authority He has because we are completely identified with Him; His authority is our authority.

† We overcome by the blood of the Lamb and the word of our testimony, and by loving not our lives unto death (Revelation 12:11). The principles of Revelation 12:11 must become our motivation.

† The enemy still attacks us and wants us to live in defeat. He attacks our minds, but we cannot be fooled into thinking there is no war or that the devil will simply leave us alone once we are in Christ. The devil is still the enemy and although we have victory, we must continue to fight in the power of the Lord, not in our own strength. We must be aggressive in our faith, appropriate what Christ did for us, and walk in His authority.

† To walk in victory, we must submit to God, resist the devil and expect him to flee from us.

The Power of Identification with Christ

Nothing is more powerful than the Cross of Jesus Christ. In this chapter, we will look at how the Cross totally defeats sin—and the power of sin—in our lives. By crucifying our old man, our unredeemed nature, the Cross brings us new life, delivering us from this evil age and breaking the world's grip on our lives. The Cross empowers us to be "dead to the law," meaning that we no longer have to perform to be accepted; and it assures us of our complete acceptance in Jesus and of the unconditional, unlimited love of our heavenly Father.

In order to more fully appropriate the power of the Cross, we must understand what it means to identify with Jesus Christ so we can understand the benefits that belong to us in Him. Romans 5:12-21 addresses the issue of identification with Christ:

> Therefore, just as through one man sin entered the world, and death through sin, and thus death spread to all men, because all sinned (For until the law sin was in the world, but sin is not imputed when there is no law. Nevertheless death reigned from Adam to Moses, even over those who had not sinned according to the likeness of the transgression of Adam, who is a type of Him who was to come. But the free gift is not like the offense. For if by the one man's offense many died, much more the grace of God and the

gift by the grace of the one Man, Jesus Christ, abounded to many. And the gift is not like that which came through the one who sinned. For the judgment which came from one offense resulted in condemnation, but the free gift which came from many offenses resulted in justification. For if by the one man's offense death reigned through the one, much more those who receive abundance of grace and of the gift of righteousness will reign in life through the One, Jesus Christ.) Therefore, as through one man's offense judgment came to all men, resulting in condemnation, even so through one Man's righteous act the free gift came to all men, resulting in justification of life. For as by one man's disobedience many were made sinners, so also by one Man's obedience many will be made righteous. Moreover the law entered that the offense might abound. But where sin abounded, grace abounded much more, so that as sin reigned in death, even so grace might reign through righteousness to eternal life through Jesus Christ our Lord.

In this passage, Paul reminds us that we are born in sin because of Adam's offense. The result of sin is always death (see Romans 6:23). Therefore, Adam's sin separated us from God and caused everyone who came after him to be born with a sinful nature. Jesus's payment for sin, at the Cross, makes it possible for all of us to be born again. Because we are born with a sin nature, we must be born again in order to be reconciled to God.

Since we are born in sin, we identify with Adam: our human nature inclines us to agree with and be in favor of sin. But when we identify with Christ, He shows us by grace that we have received His salvation and are transferred out of the Kingdom of darkness into the fullness of everything Jesus has done for us (see Colossians 1:13). We are forgiven and dead to sin.

The verses below remind us that everything Jesus did was for us. They tell us of all that belongs to us through our relationship with Him. Understanding these truths helps us identify with Christ.

> And so it is written, "The first man Adam became a living being." The last Adam [Jesus Christ] became a life-giving spirit. However, the spiritual is not first, but the natural, and afterward the spiritual. The first man was of the earth, made of dust; the second man is the Lord from heaven.
>
> 1 Corinthians 15:45-47

The New Life

What do we do with the knowledge that, in Christ, we are freely forgiven and restored to right relationship with God? Paul addresses this in Romans 6:1-5.

> What shall we say then? Shall we continue in sin that grace may abound? Certainly not! How shall we who died to sin live any longer in it? Or do you not know that as many of us as were baptized into Christ Jesus were baptized into His death? Therefore we were buried with Him through baptism into death, that just as Christ was raised from the dead by the glory of the Father, even so we also should walk in newness of life. For if we have been united together in the likeness of His death, certainly we also shall be in the likeness of His resurrection.

In Romans 6:1, Paul says we are not to continue in sin simply because grace is available to us. Instead, we must identify with Christ completely and consider ourselves dead to sin.

Identifying with Christ is a foundational issue of our faith. If we understand our identification in Adam and that we've received our sin nature from him, then we must understand our identification in Christ as we have been born again and are now found in Him. Second Corinthians 5:17 says, "Therefore, if anyone is in Christ, he is a new creation; old things have passed away; behold, all things have become new."

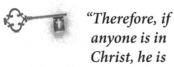

"Therefore, if anyone is in Christ, he is a new creation; old things have passed away; behold, all things have become new."

One way we express our total identification with Christ is through water baptism. Water baptism is more than a church ritual; it is something God commands as an act of faith (see Matthew 28:19; Acts 2:38). We are to be baptized in water because doing so is to follow Jesus's example (see Matthew 3:13-17). Baptism symbolizes our total rejection of any god other than the Lord Jesus and is a very serious and powerful form of identification with Him. It symbolizes the fact that we were buried with Him, were raised to new life with Him, and can now enjoy the fullness of His resurrection life. We cannot stop with salvation; God wants us to apply personally everything Jesus has done for us.

We need to remember that Romans 6:5 says, "For if we have been united together in the likeness of His death, certainly we also shall be in the likeness of His resurrection." We need to recognize that Jesus's death brought death to our sin nature, our old man. We must choose to identify with Christ and refuse to allow our sin nature to continue to rule our lives.

Because of Jesus

There are several spiritual realities that exist because of Jesus and what He has done for us:

† Our old man, sin nature, was crucified with Christ. Our sin nature is dead!

† Our old nature, which agreed with the devil, the world and the flesh, was rendered powerless.

† We are no longer slaves to sin.

Romans 6:6-8 is a powerful verse:

> Knowing this, that our old man was crucified with Him, that the body of sin might be done away with, that we should no longer be slaves of sin. For he who has died has been freed from sin. Now if we died with Christ, we believe that we shall also live with Him.

If we want to live in victory, then knowing, understanding, and comprehending the compelling truth of Romans 6:6-8 is vital. If we completely identify with Jesus's death, burial and resurrection, our old man, the body of sin, has lost its power. Our old nature is not literally "done away with," but actually "rendered inoperative." This is like having an electrical appliance that is unplugged from a power source. It is still an appliance, but it will not work unless plugged in. The same principle applies to our sin nature. Through Jesus's work on the Cross, it was "unplugged" and does not have any effect or power in our lives unless the devil can talk us into plugging it in again.

You may be like many people who say, "I just can't do this! It's too hard!" You have to realize the old nature, the old self, the body of sin, is no longer in control. You are free from the rule of your old nature. Your old nature is not gone, but if you will appropriate by faith what Jesus did at the Cross and completely identify with Him, you can live in victory over sin. Then Galatians 2:20 can become a reality in your life: "I have been crucified with Christ; it is no longer I who live, but Christ lives in me; and the life which I now live in the flesh I live by faith in the Son of God, who loved me and gave Himself for me."

Physically, you and I are descendants of the first man, Adam, who brought sin to mankind. Spiritually, we are children of God. Let's compare our identification with Adam with our new identity in Christ.

In Adam	In Christ
We are born in sin	We Are born again by the Spirit
We have death	We have life
We are separated from God	We are joined to Him
We are sinners	We are righteous; in fact, we are saints
We have a sin nature	We have a new nature
We are in agreement with sin	We now agree with God and with righteousness
Our sin nature is active	Our sin nature is rendered inoperative

Identifying ourselves in Christ is vitally important to every believer. If you think of yourself as "still a sinner", or "a sinner saved by grace," you will continue to sin. If you completely identify with Christ in His death and resurrection, you are no longer a sinner but a saint. That's right! You are a saint. You have a new nature if you identify with Christ and are born again. Remember 2 Corinthians 5:17, "...If anyone is in Christ, he is a new creation."

Let me explain this more fully. If I believe my true nature is sinful, then I will struggle with sin and live defeated in sin. My focus will be on sin. However, if I believe I am dead to sin, that I have a new nature created in Christ, and that I am the righteousness of God, then I will act differently. My focus will be on righteousness.

Now, even with a new nature, I may still sin. But I am not *a sinner;* I am simply a saint who may happen to sin. My new nature is in agreement with righteousness and is no longer in agreement with sin. God hates sin, but He loves me.

In many ways, Christians have been taught and "programmed" to believe we are still sinners and that the only reason we don't live in sin continually is that God gives us grace. This idea makes us sin-focused; it causes us to continue to live in sin; and it is not biblical.

However, when we identify with Christ, we have a new nature; our old man is rendered inoperative by the power of the Cross. We are free from living in sin and defeat. In fact, with the new nature we have in Christ, we can start focusing on our righteousness and living in victory.

Not only are we free from our old nature by the power of the Cross, but Paul tells us in Galatians 1:4 that we are delivered from this present evil age: "who gave Himself for our sins, that He might deliver us from this present evil age, according to the will of our God and Father."

This present evil age and the world system—and its powerful pull on us—have been defeated through the Cross. In addition to the wonderful fact that we are raised to life in Christ, we are also dead to the world in Him. The world system is under the rule of the enemy, but in Christ, we are no longer subject to its wickedness. In the world, people strive to "be somebody," to make money, to gain possessions and to feel worthy. This vanity lures us away from who we really are in Christ. When we are dead to the world, these empty pursuits have no power over us, as the following Scriptures prove to us:

> But God forbid that I should boast except in the Cross of our Lord Jesus Christ, by whom the world has been crucified to me, and I to the world.
>
> Galatians 6:14

> We know that we are of God, and the whole world lies under the sway of the wicked one.
>
> 1 John 5:19

> … the ruler of this world is judged.
>
> John 16:11

> These things I have spoken to you, that in Me you may have peace. In the world you will have tribulation; but be of good cheer, I have overcome the world.
>
> John 16:33

Recognizing the World's Temptations

> Do not love the world or the things in the world. If anyone loves the world, the love of the Father is not in him. For all that is in the world—the lust of the flesh, the lust of the eyes, and the pride of life—is not of the Father but is of the world.
>
> 1 John 2:15-16

The world is full of temptations, but we can be dead to them as we identify with Christ, apply His overcoming power in our lives, and appropriate His victory:

† *the lust of the flesh*: I believe this primarily affects us in the sexual areas and other extreme desires.

† *the lust of the eyes*: This is about covetousness and wanting things that we see and lust after.

† *the pride of life*: This is about "me." It tempts us to say, "I am my own boss, and nobody can tell me what to do. I do not need anything or anybody."

These three areas basically represent the temptations that are in the world. Since we have been crucified to the world, then these temptations should not rule or have control in our lives. The Bible tells us that we are to be *in* the world but not *of* the world, and these temptations are definitely "of" the world, meaning they are earthly and based in human desire; they are not of God.

"And this is the victory that has overcome the world—our faith."

> For whatever is born of God overcomes the world. And this is the victory that has overcome the world—our faith. Who is he who overcomes the world, but he who believes that Jesus is the Son of God?
>
> 1 John 5:4- 5

If this present evil age and the world are under the sway of the evil one, then we will not escape their pull and influence over us. But because of the Cross, we do not have to be subject to these dynamics either. Mark 4:18- 19 indicates that this issue is a very real problem: "Now these are the ones sown among thorns; they are the ones who hear the word, and the cares of this world, the deceitfulness of riches, and the desires for other things entering in choke the word, and it becomes unfruitful."

The cares of this world, the deceitfulness of riches, and desires for other things--all three of these are issues in this present evil age and in the world. These things can choke the God's Word and make it unfruitful in our lives. If we are not aware of these issues and their potential to ensnare us, they will affect us negatively.

Freedom from the Law

As we walk in new life through our complete identification with Jesus, we are not only dead to the world, but also dead to the law. Our righteousness is no longer based on performance, what we do or do not do. In other words, we are free from trying to be righteous by keeping rules and regulations. There is not one thing we can do to make ourselves acceptable to God. But when we receive by faith the great love and mercy, He has extended to us, we are made totally acceptable.

According to Romans 7:4, when we are in Christ, we are dead to the law because we are "married" to Him, made one with Him in the Spirit: "Therefore, my brethren, you also have become dead to the law through the body of Christ, that you may be married to another—to Him who was raised from the dead that we should bear fruit to God."

Jesus's work on the Cross forged a powerful union between us and Him. In that relationship, we love and enjoy Him in close fellowship with Him. We are united with Him, in His death and resurrection, completely identified with Him. Being dead to the law will set us free from trying to please God. All we have to do is to have our hearts right before Him and to receive and appropriate by faith the fullness of being in Christ.

Romans 7:6 says, "But now we have been delivered from the law, having died to what we were held by, so that we should serve in the newness of the Spirit and not in the oldness of the letter." In other words, we are no longer married to the law. We are free from the performance trap of trying to be good so we can be accepted and are now firmly in relationship with God. We are "married" to Him. Our acceptance is not based on our performance but His total acceptance of us. The focus is not on our works but His grace.

So we see that if we identify with Christ in His death and resurrection, our old nature is crucified. We have been delivered from the world and this present evil age. We are completely free from the law and its power as we identify with Christ.

SUMMARY

† The power of the Cross totally defeats sin and the power of sin in our lives.

† In order to more fully appropriate the power of the Cross, we must understand what it means to identify with Jesus Christ and understand the benefits that are ours in Him.

† As we identify with Christ, we identify completely with His death and completely with His risen life.

† Because of the Cross, the power of sin is broken in our lives. We are dead to sin. In Christ, our old nature is crucified and rendered inoperative.

† The power of the Cross breaks the world's hold on us.

† In Christ, we are dead to the law. We no longer need to feel that we need to perform in order to be accepted.

♥ TAKE IT TO HEART

Although it may be difficult to step back and take a serious look at certain areas of your life, God is offering you freedom and a path to overcome some of those struggles. He has made a way through the Cross for you to be made whole and be released from sins of the flesh. What are some of areas where you are being defeated, where you struggle with temptations or wrong choices? Are you under condemnation or conviction? Has the enemy bombarded your mind, will and emotions with anger, fear, rejection, lust, jealousy, pride, grief, disappointment? The answer is within reach.

🙏 TAKE IT TO GOD

Dear God,

I thank You that Your Spirit teaches me all things, guides me into all truth, is able to purify my heart and cleanse my mind. I realize that there are areas where I truly need Your healing, cleansing and forgiveness. I've tried, but I can't fix it. Please come and change my heart and my mind to be like Yours. Forgive me for all my sins and wrongdoing and bring a transformation in my life into the likeness of Christ. I willingly surrender. Now enable me to trust You and walk by the Spirit, listening to Your voice and obeying Your will. I rest in Your promises and hope for a fresh start and an empowered life.

In Jesus's name. Amen.

PART 5

Experiencing the Victorious Life

"As we comprehend and apprehend the fullness of what Jesus paid for on our behalf, we will walk in increasing wholeness, freedom and power -the resurrected life."

Living in the Power of the Cross

What does it mean to live in the power of the Cross and appropriate its truth? Let's take a journey through the Word of God and discover the amazing opportunity that each believer has to live a victorious life through the power of the Cross.

Take a moment and read through all of Romans 6, 7, and 8. These chapters will be the foundation for this chapter of *The Cross is the Key* and I will refer to a number of verses in this passage as we go along. The crucial elements are:

† We must understand what Jesus did at the Cross and how His death, burial and resurrection defeated the power of sin, setting us free from our old nature, the world and the law.

† We must completely identify with Jesus's resurrection life because He is not in the grave, but He is risen and lives forever. If we identify with His death, certainly we should identify with His resurrection.

† We must reckon ourselves dead to sin, but alive to God.

What does it mean to "reckon" ourselves dead to sin. We read about this in Romans 6:11-12: "Likewise you also, reckon yourselves to be dead indeed to sin, but alive to God in Christ Jesus our Lord. Therefore do not let sin reign in your mortal body, that you should obey it in its lusts."

To *reckon* is an accounting term that means, "to take into account, to calculate, to consider." We must literally make a decision based upon the truth of Romans 6:1-10, that our old nature was rendered inoperative and we are no longer slaves of sin. And at the same time, realize we have been transferred out of the power of sin and now completely identify with our new resurrected life "in Christ."

"We must literally say, "no" to sin and "yes" to Christ and His life."

Reflect on this: Since God's Word is true, there is tremendous power for us when we believe and act on it. Scripture tells us we must reckon ourselves dead to sin and alive to God. We must stop our old ways of thinking and fully identify with the truth of the Word and with what Jesus did on the Cross. It is time to turn from death to life in Christ. We must literally say, "no" to sin and "yes" to Christ and His life. We do all of this by faith in what Jesus has done for us.

Do not let sin reign in you anymore. If you let sin reign or have any ground in you then you are not living in accordance to the Word of God. In fact, if a person allows sin to reign or have a hold on him or her, that person is denying both the truth of God's Word and Jesus's accomplishments at the Cross.

Do you see why I say we can live in victory over sin? *We have power over sin.* Sin does *not* have power over us. As a pastor, I often hear people express that they "cannot keep from sinning." They say their bondages or problems are too hard to overcome and they just cannot stop engaging in them. When I show them this passage, most people are shocked when they read and comprehend this truth. I am not saying that exercising our God-given power over sin is easy, but the truth is that we can do it. The devil does not want us to know this truth and he certainly does not want us to apply it in our lives.

When we really appropriate this truth in our lives, we will begin to live in victory and the power of the Cross.

> And do not present your members as instruments of unrighteousness to sin, but present yourselves to God as being alive from the dead, and your members as instruments of righteousness to God.
>
> Romans 6:13

We must not allow sin to reign in us in any way. One way to keep sin far from us is to present ourselves and our "members" (our bodies, minds, senses, emotions, appetites, desires, etc.) to the Lord as instruments of righteousness. This is a command; not simply a suggestion. If we are going to appropriate everything Jesus provided for us at the Cross, we must present everything about ourselves to Him.

It is always good to present ourselves entirely to the Lord, and especially to submit those areas where we often find ourselves tempted to sin. For example, a person who struggles with visual temptation that leads to lust would want to present his or her eyes to the Lord as instruments of righteousness. That person would need to ask for God's help to look only upon things that are holy, wholesome and pure. As we present ourselves to the Lord, we become His slaves— slaves of righteousness—able to enjoy intimate relationship with Him and a victorious life in Christ.

The Problem

Even though we know the truth that we can live victoriously in Christ, the problem in our lives—the reason we struggle with the truth—is that our flesh is still alive. The old self still wants to live and reign in our lives. We may not be living in any abject sin, but our flesh, our old selfish nature still wants to have its way.

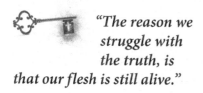

"The reason we struggle with the truth, is that our flesh is still alive."

We may know the truth of Romans 6, but many of us seem to find ourselves living in Romans 7, where Paul says he does what he doesn't want to do and he doesn't do what he wants to do.

For what I am doing, I do not understand. For what I will to do, that I do not practice; but what I hate, that I do. If, then, I do what I will not to do, I agree with the law that it is good. But now, it is no longer I who do it, but sin that dwells in me. For I know that in me (that is, in my flesh) nothing good dwells; for to will is present with me, but how to perform what is good I do not find. For the good that I will to do, I do not do; but the evil I will not to do, that I practice. Now if I do what I will not to do, it is no longer I who do it, but sin that dwells in me. I find then a law, that evil is present with me, the one who wills to do good. For I delight in the law of God according to the inward man. But I see another law in my members, warring against the law of my mind, and bringing me into captivity to the law of sin which is in my members. O wretched man that I am! Who will deliver me from this body of death?

Romans 7:15-24 (emphasis added)

If you count the use of the personal pronouns, "I," "me," and "my," which are in bold type in this passage, you will find 34! That is the problem: "I," "me," and "my" represent the flesh, our self-life. But life should not be about "me;" it should be about Jesus, who gave His life for us and now lives in us. We could be tempted to use this passage as an "excuse" for defeat, or as justification for not being able to overcome things. I don't believe that was Paul's intention in writing it. In fact, I am convinced that Paul did not live his life focused on himself; we know too much about him from his writings to believe that.

We are able to live the truths of Romans 6 through the Holy Spirit and according to the powerful truths of Romans 8. God knows we have a hard time living in the truth, so He sent His Holy Spirit to help us. As we go through some of Romans 8, you will see what I mean when I say our victory is lived out in and by the power of the Holy Spirit. It is not about our doing more or trying harder, but about yielding to the power of the Holy Spirit who gives us victory.

All of us have struggled with the flesh and failed to walk in the Spirit. But having dealt with our failures, we must then go on. The way to deal with our failures is to repent and receive the Lord's forgiveness. We must then believe we are not condemned, but fully forgiven and free, according to Romans 8:1-4:

> There is therefore now no condemnation to those who are in Christ Jesus, who do not walk according to the flesh, but according to the Spirit. For the law of the Spirit of life in Christ Jesus has made me free from the law of sin and death. For what the law could not do in that it was weak through the flesh, God did by sending His own Son in the likeness of sinful flesh, on account of sin: He condemned sin in the flesh, that the righteous requirement of the law might be fulfilled in us who do not walk according to the flesh but according to the Spirit.

If we are in Christ, the shame, guilt and condemnation of sin have no place in our lives. We are free! We are still subject to the conviction of the Holy Spirit, but not to the condemnation of the enemy. The Holy Spirit will point to a sinful attitude or behavior and say, *"That* is sin." The enemy will point to you and say, *"You* are a sinner." We respond to the Holy Spirit's conviction with repentance, but we feel shame in response to the condemnation of the enemy. Understanding the difference between condemnation and conviction of sin is vitally important to living a victorious life.

The devil condemns you as a person and tells you that you are a failure. The Holy Spirit will convict you of sin, pointing out the sinful attitude or action but never condemns you as a person. He loves you but He hates sin. The devil just hates you, but he loves the sin. See the difference?

"In the Spirit, there is no condemnation for you, no matter what you have done or failed to do."

In Christ, you are free. You must appropriate this prevailing truth if you are going to walk in the Spirit. There is no condemnation for you, no matter what you have done or have failed to do, regardless of what you have said or thought. Once you repent and put your sins under the blood of Jesus, you are cleansed and forgiven.

The Keys to Victory

> For those who live according to the flesh set their minds on the things of the flesh, but those who live according to the Spirit, the things of the Spirit. For to be carnally minded is death, but to be spiritually minded is life and peace. Because the carnal mind is enmity against God; for it is not subject to the law of God, nor indeed can be. So then, those who are in the flesh cannot please God.
>
> Romans 8:5-8

The enemy so often attacks us on the battleground of the mind, so we must be diligent to guard our thoughts. The enemy knows if he can get us to think negative thoughts—to focus on ourselves, our problems and disappointments, our circumstances or the things we do not understand—he can turn us away from the Lord and the things of the Spirit. The negative, carnal thoughts the enemy brings to our minds will always produce death.

We must be diligent to guard our minds against thoughts the enemy would use against us. He knows the mind set on the flesh is death and he is determined to bring death to us (see Romans 8:6). He wants, and aggressively seeks, control of our minds. We must not allow thoughts to run rampant in our minds or allow ourselves to focus mentally on anything that "exalts itself against the knowledge of God" (2 Corinthians 10:5). If we do, our minds will be set on the flesh and death will result.

In order to gain victory in our minds, we must faithfully obey 2 Corinthians 10:5 and bring "every thought into captivity to the obedience of Christ." We must set our minds upon the Spirit and upon the things of God. We must continually focus on who Jesus is and what He did for us at the Cross.

Second Corinthians 10:3-5 acknowledges the battle of the mind and gives us instructions for winning it:

"Knowing Scriptures enables us to identify the lies of the enemy."

> For though we walk in the flesh, we do not war according to the flesh. For the weapons of our warfare are not carnal, but mighty in God for pulling down strongholds, casting down arguments and every high thing that exalts itself against the knowledge of God, bringing every thought into captivity to the obedience of Christ.

The only way we can take thoughts captive is to renew our minds with the Word of God. The more time we spend in the Word and really understand it, the more our minds will be renewed. Knowing the Scriptures enables us to identify the lies of the enemy that are clearly contrary to God's Word. If we do not know the Word of God, taking our thoughts captive will be impossible.

Talking about knowing the truth of God's Word reminds me of the story I once heard about the way the FBI trains its agents to detect counterfeit bills. They do not study all the different types of counterfeit currency and focus on what is wrong with counterfeit bills. Instead, they focus on examining only the original, legitimate bills. Every ounce of their energy goes into fully knowing true currency. We need to operate the same way in our lives. Putting every ounce of our energy into fully knowing the true Word of God is the only way to avoid being led astray by counterfeit "truths" and the twisted lies of the enemy.

> Set your mind on things above, not on things on the earth.
>
> Colossians 3:2

The key to victory in the battle of the mind is to set our minds on the things of the Spirit, the "things above." As we do, peace will come, because Isaiah 26:3 says, "You will keep him in perfect peace whose mind is stayed on You, because he trusts in You." Circumstances may not change, but we will not be focusing on them. We will be thinking about Jesus, the One who never changes (see Hebrews 13:8). He is totally victorious, and He has secured our victory.

Take a close look at Romans 8:9-14. In this passage, you will see that the only way to live in the Spirit and keep your mind set on things above is by the power of the Spirit. The power of the Cross is released in our lives by the Spirit. In our own strength, we cannot overcome; but Jesus has *already* overcome and we are in Him. He has given us the Holy Spirit so that we might walk in the victory He has won. He lives in us and ministers His victory by the Spirit.

Romans 8:11 teaches us that the Spirit who raised Jesus from the dead lives in us to give life to our mortal bodies. This is great news! Since this is true, why don't we allow the Holy Spirit to really help us? If He can raise Jesus from the grave, I believe He has enough power to help us overcome a defeated enemy. Romans 8:15-17 says:

> For you did not receive the spirit of bondage again to fear, but you received the Spirit of adoption by whom we cry out, "Abba, Father." The Spirit Himself bears witness with our spirit that we are children of God, and if children, then heirs—heirs of God and joint heirs with Christ, if indeed we suffer with Him, that we also may be glorified together.

The Holy Spirit wants to lead us into an intimate, personal relationship with God. He is the "Spirit of adoption," who has been given so we will have a life-changing revelation of the Father's love for us. He establishes our true identity as children of God. The Holy Spirit empowers us and leads us to live in the fullness of our position as children of God—heirs of everything Jesus purchased for us at the Cross (see Romans 8:14).

If you struggle in any of these areas, ask the Holy Spirit to help you. He is the Helper, the One God sent to assist us as we grow in His love and power.

SUMMARY

† The truth of Romans 6 is accomplished in and by the Holy Spirit, who lives within us, according to Romans 8. The objective truth is subjectively lived out as we depend upon the Holy Spirit. He is the power of God, given to us to help us live and be everything God's Word says we are.

† A battle is raging. Our old man, the body of sin, the flesh, wants to rule us. It has been rendered inoperative, but still tries to live and fight against the Spirit of God.

† To live in the power of the Cross, we must:

  › reckon the old nature dead.

  › recognize that the power of our sinful nature was buried with Christ.

  › identify completely with Jesus's death, burial and resurrection.

  › not let sin continue to rule and reign in us.

  › realize that we now have the power over sin, the flesh and our old nature.

  › present our members to God as instruments of righteousness.

  › not live in Romans 7:15-24 and make excuses for defeat.

  › live in and by the Holy Spirit, in Romans 8.

  › refuse condemnation.

  › live and walk by the Spirit.

➤ renew our minds so we can take thoughts captive and win the battle of the mind.

➤ receive the Spirit of adoption, God's love and His acceptance. Know we are children of God and joint heirs with Jesus.

13

The Resurrected Life

Everything in the Bible, every promise, belongs to us because Jesus Christ purchased it with His life for us at Calvary. Believing this in our hearts is the key to our receiving it in our lives personally. As we comprehend and apprehend the fullness of what Jesus paid for on our behalf, we will walk in increasing wholeness, freedom and power—the resurrected life. If we are going to appropriate all Jesus did at the Cross, we must daily live the Cross. What that means for every believer is:

1. *We must believe what Jesus did on the Cross was a complete and eternal work.* It forever separated us from sin; it severed us from our old nature and broke the enemy's power over our lives. Through the Cross, we have been given everything we need to live in victory.

2. *We must see ourselves as dead to sin*—dead to our old lives and dead to our old ways of thinking. We must see ourselves alive to God. What happened at the Cross was an exchange. We must train ourselves to reckon our old selves dead and understand that we are now alive to God so we can truly have life.

3. *We must identify completely with the resurrection.* Jesus Christ is not dead. He lives and because He lives, we live. Tremendous resurrection power is available to us. There is no reason for us to continually live defeated lives. Of course, we will be challenged; but because of what Jesus did on the Cross, we need not live in

constant defeat. At Calvary, He paid in full the price for us to have victory in every area of our lives.

4. *We must receive and trust in the Holy Spirit to empower and help us.* As we saw in Chapter 12, the Holy Spirit helps us live in victory.

At the Cross, Jesus Christ forever secured our victory over every situation we could ever face. Despite this unchangeable truth, many people still struggle to appropriate and fully live in the power of everything He provided. Why is this? How can we begin to experience the fullness of His provision?

Let's look at what Jesus said to His disciples as He explained what is necessary in order to follow Him completely, which will result in being able to live in the power of the Cross:

> Then Jesus said to His disciples, "If anyone desires to come after Me, let him deny himself, and take up his cross, and follow Me. For whoever desires to save his life will lose it, but whoever loses his life for My sake will find it."
>
> Matthew 16:24- 25

What is Jesus asking us to do in this Scripture? *"If anyone desires to come after Me ..."* Do you really desire to follow Jesus? Do you really want to be free and live in the victory and power of the Cross? It will cost you. Some people, had they known from the beginning that following Jesus would cost them and that they would have to *deny* themselves, would not want to pay the price. But after seeing the glorious victory and wonderful relationship we can have now with Jesus, I hope and pray that you see that "losing our lives" (our souls) is nothing compared to gaining *everything* in Christ. In Him, we gain life eternal, forever living in the presence of the King of kings and Lord of lords.

"Let him deny himself ..." How do we deny ourselves? Basically, we deny ourselves when we choose to live our lives according to the

Word of God. We change the way we think about things the moment we realize that our natural thinking is contrary to the Word. We bring our emotions under control when we see that they want to run our lives and take us away from living according to the Word. We submit our wills and choose to obey the Word even when we think we are right.

Every time your soul, your self-life, wants to rule, you must deny it and obey God. This doesn't mean denying *who* you are but denying the desires of your mind or flesh that don't line up with God's will.

Instead of living as subjects of our souls (mind, emotions and will), we must take our souls to the Cross and allow soulish manifestations to be crucified there. We must reckon them dead so they cannot rule over us. Thereby, we will be free to follow Christ and allow Him to reign in our lives.

We may struggle daily or even moment-by-moment to overcome our minds, wills and/or emotions; they will always want to control us. By the power of the Spirit, we must master the soul so we can freely submit to the Lord, allow Him to lead us and live in the victory of the Cross.

If we are going to be disciples of Jesus and live the resurrection life, we must understand that we must walk according to Matthew 16:24, 25. The word *life* in Matthew 16:25 means, "soul"—the mind, will and emotions, which must be brought under the submission of the spirit.

The soul possesses its own "self-life," which prohibits the life of the spirit and produces death. The mind, the will and the emotions tend to be opposed to God's Word and to His Spirit, striving instead to live in a person and "rule" that person. Because this is contrary to the truth of God's Word, the soul must be put to death. We must deny our souls and not allow them to have power over our lives (see Matthew 16:25).

This soulish life is where the flesh is manifested. We saw in Chapter 12 that the flesh wants to rule and reign; and it does rule and reign when our souls are "leading" our lives instead of our spirits. So, how does the soul—our mind, will and emotions—try to rule our lives?

Our Minds...

When we let our minds run our lives, they always want to know and understand before they can receive anything. In western culture, where Greek thinking influences us so heavily, we crave intellectual understanding. In fact, we equate understanding something with being able to live it out in our lives. We can agree with our minds about the truth of God's Word, but that does not necessarily mean we will act upon it. When our minds rule us, we approach almost everything in life from an intellectual perspective.

Our Emotions...

Some of us are led by our emotions. Emotions get inflamed and we have high "highs" and low "lows." We allow our feelings to drive or control us and influence our decisions. When this happens, the devil can have free reign in our lives as he causes us to be tossed to and fro by everything that happens. When things are going well, we feel good, but when things are not going well, we are down and defeated. Our emotions can be unreliable and will very often lead us the wrong way.

"Our emotions can be unreliable and will very often lead us the wrong way."

Our Will...

I am sure you've heard the phrase, "strong-willed" in reference to people who will not be moved from their positions or opinions. Once they determine they are right they will not change or adjust. Stubbornness is as the sin of iniquity and idolatry (1 Samuel 15:22). When we determine we are right and refuse to move from a certain position even though we may be wrong, we have set ourselves up as our own gods. This is idolatry because it exalts our own opinions over the truth of God.

The human soul is not inherently evil, but it must come under the rule of the spirit, which is subject to the Holy Spirit. We are spirit beings who are to be led by the Spirit of God. We have a soul (mind, will, and emotions) that lives in our bodies.

The spirit of a believer is born again and it should be in charge; the soul is being saved and is in a process of learning to yield to our spirit and the Holy Spirit: our bodies will be saved eventually. Understanding the relationship between the spirit, the soul and the body is essential to maturing in Christ. We have to learn to submit our souls and our bodies to our spirits, which are led by the Holy Spirit.

Unfortunately, many people allow either their bodies or their physical appetites, which are subject to this world system, to lead them. We looked at the world system in a Chapter 11, when I mentioned the lust of the flesh, lust of the eyes and the pride of life. All of these affect our physical bodies. When we allow such things to govern us, we will live in defeat.

The Importance of Forgiveness

One of the best examples of the battle we face and one of the most important issues we deal with is forgiving those who have hurt us. Everyone gets hurt and offended by other people. Sadly, the people closest to us are usually the ones who do the most to hurt and offend us. Our parents, spouses, children, friends, church friends, and work associates are the ones with whom we are often in close relationship—

and they are usually the ones we have problems with along the way. Casual relationships come and go, and for that reason, they usually do not have the potential to hurt us as our close relationships do.

When someone we love hurts or offends us, we have a decision to make: We can become angry and harbor unforgiveness, or we can choose to forgive. If we choose to hold on to the offense and not to forgive, then we become bitter and we actually open a door to the enemy to work in our lives (Matthew 18:21-35). Ephesians 6:12 tells us that we do not wrestle against people but against the spiritual forces of wickedness. The enemy's scheme is to cause us to be angry with one another and to harbor unforgiveness toward others in our hearts so that we give him legal access to harass us.

"Our forgiveness from God is directly tied to our forgiving others."

Matthew 6:12, 14-15 clearly states that our forgiveness from God is directly tied to our forgiving others. This is another key to our victory.

When we are offended, our self-life (our flesh, our soul) wants to exact revenge on those who hurt us. As I said before, everyone has to deal with hurts and offenses. But if we are going to deny ourselves, we must give up what we think is our "right" for revenge. We must choose to obey the Word and forgive from the heart those who hurt and offend us. Our minds will say, "What happened to you was not fair! It just wasn't right!" This may be true, but that has no bearing on the truth of God's Word and His direct command to forgive.

If our emotions become inflamed and we really get angry, it is very hard to forgive. If we are really hurt and offended, our mind justifies our right to be angry, our emotions get inflamed and we decide with our will that someone has to pay. People tell me they "just can't" forgive what was done to them. They think forgiveness is a feeling. It isn't a feeling; it's a choice to obey God's Word.

But the Bible says we must forgive. Forgiveness is love in action. Jesus modeled this for us at the Cross, when He forgave those who crucified Him. In actuality, He forgave all of us forever. His forgiveness at the Cross was the supreme act of love. Because He forgave us, we must forgive those who hurt or offend us. In fact, because He has forgiven us, we *can* forgive everyone who has hurt or offended us.

When we choose to forgive in obedience to God's Word, we are choosing to extend love and we are denying ourselves and our rights. When we forgive, we are not saying that people did not hurt us or that we agree with what they did. We are simply choosing to deny our souls (the self-life) and walk by the Spirit in love and forgiveness.

I have counseled many people who struggle with unforgiveness. Time after time, I hear the same thing, "I just cannot forgive So-and-So." And time after time, I go through the same explanation I have shared in this chapter to help people walk in love and forgiveness. It's true, forgiveness is not easy, but we can do it. I have seen hundreds of people choose to deny themselves, for-

"On the other side of the choice to forgive are amazing testimonies.."

give those who have hurt and offended them and receive freedom and healing. Their lives on the other side of the *choice* to forgive are amazing testimonies to the power of God when they simply choose to walk in obedience to His command to forgive.

Pick Up Your Cross Daily

It is imperative to pick up your cross daily. The Cross not only represents all that Jesus did for us, but also represents every place where your will intersects with, or crosses, His will. Again, every time we deny your soul the chance to rule over you and choose to obey His will, you are picking up your cross and following Jesus.

This is what true disciples of Jesus do. They deny their souls (self-life, flesh) and pick up their crosses in obedience to God's Word, and they follow Jesus in love. Every time we choose to let our soul or self-life rule and reign, we lay down our cross and stop following Jesus. Every time we choose to excuse ourselves from sinful behavior, try to defend ourselves, or try to protect ourselves, we are coming down from the cross and choosing our way instead of Jesus's way. The same is true when we refuse to accept responsibility for our sinful actions and blame others. Criticism and talking about others are also sin and these are other ways we choose to exalt ourselves instead of denying ourselves.

I could go on and on with examples of times we can choose the self-life over denying ourselves and following Jesus. Every time we fail to deny ourselves, our soul gets stronger as we deny the message of the Cross, which is the power of God. I don't know about you, but I don't want my soul to get stronger; I don't want to deny the message of the Cross! I want to proclaim it loudly and let my spirit win the war over my soul and my body.

If we do not deny ourselves and take up our cross, we allow our flesh to become stronger and stronger. Notice what Galatians 5:13-18 says:

> For you, brethren, have been called to liberty; only do not use liberty as an opportunity for the flesh, but through love serve one another. For all the law is fulfilled in one word,

even in this: "You shall love your neighbor as yourself." But if you bite and devour one another, beware lest you be consumed by one another! I say then: Walk in the Spirit, and you shall not fulfill the lust of the flesh. For the flesh lusts against the Spirit, and the Spirit against the flesh; and these are contrary to one another, so that you do not do the things that you wish. But if you are led by the Spirit, you are not under the law.

As you can see from this passage in Galatians, we have been called to liberty but we must be careful of the flesh. We must love one another.

This passage warns that if we bite and devour one another we will be consumed by one another. People have told me they just don't understand why others are so spiteful to them and treat them so badly. After a little investigation, I usually discover this is exactly how those people treat others! They are living proof of Matthew 7:2, "For with what judgment you judge, you will be judged; and with the measure you use, it will be measured back to you."

So what do we do when others hurt, offend or treat us badly? We walk in the Spirit, choosing to forgive, choosing to deny our souls, our self-life. In other words, we choose not to carry out the deeds of the flesh (see Galatians 5:19-21), which are outward manifestations of not walking in the Spirit.

Notice the rewards of walking in the Spirit as these verses continue:

But the fruit of the Spirit is love, joy, peace, longsuffering, kindness, goodness, faithfulness, gentleness, self-control. Against such there is no law. And those who are Christ's have crucified the flesh with its passions and desires. If we live in the Spirit, let us also walk in the Spirit.

Galatians 5:22-25

This does not say the *fruits* of the Spirit. Actually, the "fruit of the Spirit" is singular! We are empowered to walk in and exhibit all of this fruit, not just some of it. If we walk in the Spirit, the qualities listed in Galatians 5:22-25, can individually and collectively be ours; we are filled with and exhibit the spiritual fruit in our lives. Life springs up in us and in those around us. This is the beautiful message of the Cross and the power of God.

SUMMARY

† We must believe that what Jesus did at the Cross was a complete, eternal work. We need to see ourselves as dead to sin; identify completely with the resurrection; and receive and trust in the Holy Spirit to empower us and help us.

† We want to follow Christ in victory! This means overcoming the soulish life in which the self (our mind, emotions, and will) is manifested. Our souls are not evil, but they must be subject to the rule of our spirits, which are subject to the Holy Spirit. In a believer, the spirit is born again and should be in charge.

† We must understand the importance of forgiveness. Forgiveness is love in action and requires that we deny ourselves and walk by the Spirit.

† We need to realize that the flesh wars against the spirit. If we don't deny ourselves, the flesh gets stronger and the fruit of the Spirit gets weaker. We need to exhibit the fruit of the Spirit, because those qualities are the product of a crucified life.

♥ TAKE IT TO HEART

Many Christians, even though they are sincerely committed to following Christ, continue to live in unforgiveness and are not walking by the Spirit. They struggle with areas of weakness and find themselves powerless to overcome and even obey God's commands. The Word of God makes it clear that through Jesus's work on the Cross, we have been given all that we need to lay aside these things of the world and walk in freedom, holiness, and life. It's through the power of the Holy Spirit. God's desire is that we enjoy Him and then those around us are recipients of His love and all the fruit of the Spirit operating in our lives—that we would be blessed in order to be a blessing. Have you appropriated the work of the Cross in your life? Reckoned yourself dead to sin and put aside the deeds of the flesh? Have you identified with Christ? Are you walking in the fruit of peace, patience, kindness, goodness and all the beauty of a life set apart unto Him? He offers you true freedom to live a holy, blessed, sanctified life—through the Power of the Cross.

🙏 TAKE IT TO GOD

Dear God,

Would You please come now to search my heart and reveal any unforgiveness in those areas where I am not walking in the fruit of the Spirit or Your ways, reckoning myself dead to the law, the world and sin. I do want to be made righteous and become more like Jesus. I want my life to be a representation of who You truly are. I ask that Your Holy Spirit come and guide me into all truth and show me the way that pleases You. I choose to lay aside those things which hinder my life of holiness and fruitfulness and joy in your Kingdom. And now, by faith, I receive all that You have done for me through and in the powerful name of Jesus.

Amen.

The Cross and Communion

O ne of the greatest and most meaningful ways to appropriate the Cross in our lives is through taking communion (also called the Lord's Supper or the Eucharist). It is participating in the Lord's table, on a regular basis, as Scripture instructs us to do, or setting aside time in your home to observe personal communion. The reason why communion is so important is that it reminds us of all that Jesus did at the Cross on our behalf—a work that is truly overwhelming when we stop and think about it. Through Christ's broken body, we have *everything*. Physically partaking of the representative bread and wine, meditating on His sacrifice and focusing on His body which was broken for us and His blood which was shed, brings us into a deeper understanding of the enormity and weight of the Cross He bore. We come to understand, in measure, and value the truth that it is "Christ in you, the hope of glory!" (Colossians 1:27).

In Remembrance of Jesus

For I received from the Lord that which I also delivered to you: that the Lord Jesus on the same night in which He was betrayed took bread; and when He had given thanks, He broke it and said, "Take, eat; this is My body which is broken for you; do this in remembrance of Me." In the same manner He also took the cup after supper, saying, "This cup is the new covenant in My blood. This do, as often as you drink it, in remembrance of Me." For as often as you eat this

bread and drink this cup, you proclaim the Lord's death till
He comes.

1 Corinthians 11:23-26

When we take communion, we are told to do so in remembrance
of Jesus. If we will do this on a regular basis, we will be continually
reminded of the cost Jesus paid at the Cross and the awesome benefits He intended for us there. This is one way we can appropriate the
blessings and benefits of the Cross in our lives. Taking communion
refocuses and realigns us with Jesus. It can be done collectively (as in
a worship service) and/or privately (in our homes).

However, this Scripture makes clear that taking the bread or the cup
unworthily is a serious issue. If we eat the bread and drink this cup
in an unworthy manner, we are guilty of the body and blood of the
Lord; we are judging ourselves and failing to discern the powerful
truth of His body. In fact, if we do eat and drink without appropriating and remembering all Jesus did at the Cross, we can literally
become sick and die, according to verse 30.

> Therefore whoever eats this bread or drinks this cup of the
> Lord in an unworthy manner will be guilty of the body and
> blood of the Lord. But let a man examine himself, and so
> let him eat of the bread and drink of the cup. For he who
> eats and drinks in an unworthy manner eats and drinks
> judgment to himself, not discerning the Lord's body. For this
> reason many are weak and sick among you, and many sleep.
>
> 1 Corinthians 11:27-30

On the other hand, if we do partake in a worthy manner—cleansing
ourselves, forgiving others, and believing in all that Jesus did at the
Cross—then it will produce health and life. If one is true, the oppo-
site must be true too.

I want to encourage you to never allow communion to become a mere routine occurrence or simply a religious event. Take communion often. Keep the truth of all the benefits and blessings of Jesus's work on the Cross in your mind every time you take this meal. Remember the awesome love of the Father and the love of the Son who paid with His life so you could have life eternal. Reflect upon the message of the power of the Cross. God loved you enough to make such an unfathomable sacrifice for you!

SUMMARY

† Taking communion is a great and practical way to appropriate the Cross in your life. It will help you remember what Jesus did on the Cross and doing so refocuses and realigns you with Christ.

† Examine yourself before taking the bread and the cup, so you can partake in a worthy manner. Take time to forgive others and cleanse yourself before taking communion. Otherwise, you eat and drink judgment to yourself and are not discerning the Lord's body.

† Take communion so you can appropriate in your life the blessings and benefits that Christ intends for you to have. You may be overwhelmed when you think of what He did and why He did it but focusing on it will bring power to your life.

† Taking communion can be done corporately, as in a worship service, or privately, in your own home or with your family or friends. Either way, you are remembering what Christ did for you.

A WORD FROM THE AUTHOR

I hope and pray this book has blessed and encouraged you to believe that "the Cross is the key" to victorious living in Christ. Jesus died a horrible death so we could be free from sin and death and join Him in His resurrected life. All of the benefits of His life are available for us today! The key lessons in this book are:

1. The Cross represents the awesome love of God.

✝ He loved us so much He gave His only begotten Son to die for us.

✝ Even while we were sinners, Christ died for us.

✝ He loved us first because God is love.

2. Through the Cross we are:

✝ redeemed.

✝ forgiven.

✝ made righteous.

✝ justified.

✝ reconciled to God.

✝ adopted into the family of God.

✝ made a child of God.

✝ made joint heirs with Jesus.

3. Through the Cross we received an inheritance, the "exchange of the Cross."

+ Jesus was punished so we could be forgiven.

+ He was made sin with our sinfulness so we could be made the righteousness of God.

+ He was rejected so we could be accepted in the Beloved.

+ He was cut off by death so we could be joined to God.

+ He bore our shame so we could share in His glory.

+ He was wounded so we could be healed.

+ He became poor so we could share in His abundance.

+ He became a curse so we could receive the blessing of Abraham.

+ He died our death so we could share His life.

+ He was buried so we could be raised to walk in newness of life.

4. We receive all of God's promises through faith.

+ Faith comes by hearing the Word.

+ Faith also comes as we look unto Jesus, the author and finisher of our faith.

5. Through the Cross, Jesus completely defeated the enemy and made a public spectacle of his defeat.

+ Because of this victory, we can also live in victory.

+ Jesus was raised from the dead through the power of the Holy Spirit, and we have the same Holy Spirit living in us.

6. Through the power of the Cross and our complete identification with the death, burial and resurrection of Jesus.

† Our old nature was rendered inoperative.

† We are crucified to the power of the world and the power of the law.

† We must reckon ourselves dead to sin and alive to God and present ourselves as slaves of God.

7. Through the power of the Cross, we must live the Cross daily.

† If we want to follow Jesus, we must deny ourselves and take up our cross daily. We must not let our souls (minds, wills and emotions) rule our lives, but we must walk in the Spirit.

† The walk of the Cross is where our will crosses God's will.

† In every situation we must choose to obey His will.

8. Communion brings us to focus on the Cross.

† When we take communion, we are reminded of the power of the Cross and all Jesus did for us at the Cross.

† Take communion often and allow the benefits of communion overwhelm you.

IN CLOSING ...

For the message of the Cross is foolishness to those who are perishing, but to us who are being saved it is the power of God.
1 Corinthians 1:18

As I wrote in the beginning of this book, my prayer is that every time you see a Cross or anything that reminds you of a Cross, you will remember the awesome love of the Father who loved you so much that He gave His Son, His Beloved Son, to die for you. Always remember the benefits and blessings we have because of the Cross and be reminded that the message of the **Cross** is the power of God and the **Key** to victorious living!

Powerful Truths from the Word of God

God's Word is full of powerful truths about the Cross, the love of God, God's Word, and other subjects addressed in this book. These Scriptures were chosen specifically to help bring transformation to your life or anyone's who will meditate on them and apply them in personal, practical ways. I encourage you to read and meditate on them often and make them the foundation of your walk with God and your daily living.

"For the life of the flesh is in the blood, and I have given it to you upon the altar to make atonement for your souls; for it is the blood that makes atonement for the soul." Leviticus 17:11

"This Book of the Law shall not depart from your mouth, but you shall meditate in it day and night, that you may observe to do according to all that is written in it. For then you will make your way prosperous, and then you will have good success." Joshua 1:8

"Blessed is the man who walks not in the counsel of the ungodly, nor stands in the path of sinners, nor sits in the seat of the scornful; but his delight is in the law of the Lord, and in His law he meditates day and night. He shall be like a tree planted by the rivers of water, that brings forth its fruit in its season, whose leaf also shall not wither; and whatever he does shall prosper." Psalms 1:1-3

You will keep him in perfect peace whose mind is stayed on You, because he trusts in You.

Isaiah 26:3

He is despised and rejected by men, a Man of sorrows and acquainted with grief. And we hid, as it were, our faces from Him; He was despised, and we did not esteem Him. Surely He has borne our griefs and carried our sorrows; yet we esteemed Him stricken, smitten by God, and afflicted. But He was wounded for our transgressions, He was bruised for our iniquities; the chastisement for our peace was upon Him, and by His stripes we are healed.

Isaiah 53:3-5

"For He was cut off from the land of the living; for the transgressions of My people He was stricken.

Isaiah 53:8

Yet it pleased the Lord to bruise Him; He has put Him to grief. When you make His soul an offering for sin ...

Isaiah 53:10

Instead of your shame you shall have double honor, and instead of confusion they shall rejoice in their portion. Therefore in their land they shall possess double; everlasting joy shall be theirs.

Isaiah 61:7

When evening had come, they brought to Him many who were demon-possessed. And He cast out the spirits with a word, and healed all who were sick, that it might be fulfilled which was spoken by Isaiah.

Matthew 8:16- 17

Then Jesus said to His disciples, "If anyone desires to come after Me, let him deny himself, and take up his cross, and follow Me. For whoever desires to save his life will lose it, but whoever loses his life for My sake will find it."

Matthew 16:24- 25

I say to you, if you have faith as a mustard seed, you will say to this mountain, "Move from here to there," and it will move; and nothing will be impossible for you.

Matthew 17:20

And Jesus cried out again with a loud voice and yielded up His spirit. Then, behold, the veil of the temple was torn in two from top to bottom; and the earth quaked, and the rocks were split, and the graves were opened; and many bodies of the saints who had fallen asleep were raised; and coming out of the graves after His resurrection, they went into the holy city and appeared to many. So when the centurion and those with him, who were guarding Jesus, saw the earthquake and the things that had happened, they feared greatly, saying, "Truly this was the Son of God!"

Matthew 27:50-54

And Jesus came and spoke to them, saying, "All authority has been given to Me in heaven and on earth. Go therefore and make disciples of all the nations, baptizing them in the name of the Father and of the Son and of the Holy Spirit, teaching them to observe all things that I have commanded you; and lo, I am with you always, even to the end of the age." Amen.

Matthew 28:18-20

When all the people were baptized, it came to pass that Jesus also was baptized; and while He prayed, the heaven was opened. And the Holy Spirit descended in bodily form like a dove upon Him, and a voice came from heaven which said, "You are My beloved Son; in You I am well pleased."

Luke 3:21-22

Then the seventy returned with joy, saying, "Lord, even the demons are subject to us in Your name.' And He said to them, 'I saw Satan fall like lightening from heaven. Behold, I give you the authority to trample on serpents and scorpions, and over all the power of the enemy, and nothing shall by any means hurt you. Nevertheless do not rejoice in this, that the spirits are subject to you, but rather rejoice because your names are written in heaven."

Luke 10:17-20

Why do you seek the living among the dead? He is not here, but is risen!

Luke 24:5-6

Behold, the Lamb of God who takes away the sin of the world!

John 1:29

For God so loved the world that He gave His only begotten Son, that whoever believes in Him should not perish but have everlasting life.

John 3:16

He who believes in the Son has everlasting life; and he who does not believe the Son shall not see life, but the wrath of God abides on him.

John 3:36

If you abide in My word, you are My disciples indeed.

John 8:31

Jesus said to her, "I am the resurrection and the life. He who believes in Me, though he may die, he shall live. And whoever lives and believes in Me shall never die. Do you believe this?"

John 11:25- 26

And when He has come, He will convict the world of sin, and of righteousness, and of judgment: of sin, because they do not believe in Me; of righteousness, because I go to My Father and you see Me no more; of judgment, because the ruler of this world is judged.

John 16:8-11

Most assuredly, I say to you that you will weep and lament, but the world will rejoice; and you will be sorrowful, but your sorrow will be turned into joy.

John 16:20

These things I have spoken to you, that in Me you may have peace. In the world you will have tribulation; but be of good cheer, I have overcome the world.

John 16:33

But you shall receive power when the Holy Spirit has come upon you; and you shall be witnesses to Me in Jerusalem, and in all Judea and Samaria, and to the ends of the earth.

Acts 1:8

Men of Israel, hear these words: Jesus of Nazareth, a Man attested by God to you by miracles, wonders, and signs which God did through Him in your midst, as you your-selves also know—Him, being delivered by the determined purpose and foreknowledge of God, you have taken by lawless hands, have crucified, and put to death; whom God raised up, having loosed the pains of death, because it was not possible that He should be held by it.

Acts 2:22-24

And though they found no cause for death in Him, they asked Pilate that He should be put to death. Now when they had fulfilled all that was written concerning Him, they took Him down from the tree and laid Him in a tomb. But God raised Him from the dead.

Acts 13:28-30

For in Him we live and move and have our being ...

Acts 17:28

Being justified freely by His grace through the redemption that is in Christ Jesus, whom God sent forth as a propitiation by His blood, through faith, to demonstrate His righteousness, because in His forbearance God had passed over the sins that were previously committed, to demonstrate at the present time His righteousness, that He might be just and the justifier of the one who has faith in Jesus.

Romans 3:24-26

For the promise that he would be the heir of the world was not to Abraham or to his seed through the law, but through the righteousness of faith.

Romans 4:13

(as it is written, "I have made you a father of many nations") in the presence of Him whom he believed—God, who gives life to the dead and calls those things which do not exist as though they did; who, contrary to hope, in hope believed ...

Romans 4:17- 18

He did not waver at the promise of God through unbelief, but was strengthened in faith, giving glory to God, and being fully convinced that what He had promised He was also able to perform.

Romans 4:20- 21

Now it was not written for his sake alone that it was imputed to Him, but also for us. It shall be imputed to us who believe in Him who raised up Jesus our Lord from the dead, who was delivered up because of our offenses, and was raised because of our justification.

Romans 4:23-25

Now hope does not disappoint, because the love of God has been poured out in our hearts by the Holy Spirit who was given to us.

Romans 5:5

For when we were still without strength, in due time Christ died for the ungodly.

Romans 5:6

But God demonstrates His own love toward us, in that while we were still sinners, Christ died for us. Much more then, having now been justified by His blood, we shall be saved from wrath through Him. For if when we were enemies we were reconciled to God through the death of His Son, much more, having been reconciled, we shall be saved by His life.

Romans 5:8-10

What shall we say then? Shall we continue in sin that grace may abound? Certainly not! How shall we who died to sin live any longer in it? Or do you not know that as many of us as were baptized into Christ Jesus were baptized into

His death? Therefore we were buried with Him through baptism into death, that just as Christ was raised from the dead by the glory of the Father, even so we also should walk in newness of life. For if we have been united together in the likeness of His death, certainly we also shall be in the likeness of His resurrection.

Romans 6:1-5

Knowing this, that our old man was crucified with Him, that the body of sin might be done away with, that we should no longer be slaves of sin. For he who has died has been freed from sin. Now if we died with Christ, we believe that we shall also live with Him.

Romans 6:6-8

Likewise you also, reckon yourselves to be dead indeed to sin, but alive to God in Christ Jesus our Lord. Therefore do not let sin reign in your mortal body, that you should obey it in its lusts.

Romans 6:11-12

*Therefore, my brethren, you also have become dead to the law through the body of Christ, that you may be married to another—to Him who was raised f*rom the dead that we should bear fruit to God.

Romans 7:4

But now we have been delivered from the law, having died to what we were held by, so that we should serve in the newness of the Spirit and not in the oldness of the letter

Romans 7:6

There is therefore now no condemnation to those who are in Christ Jesus, who do not walk according to the flesh, but according to the Spirit. For the law of the Spirit of life in Christ Jesus has made me free from the law of sin and death. For what the law could not do in that it was weak through the flesh, God did by sending His own Son in the likeness of sinful flesh, on account of sin: He condemned sin in the flesh, that the righteous requirement of the law might be fulfilled in us who do not walk according to the flesh but according to the Spirit.

Romans 8:1-4

For to be carnally minded is death, but to be spiritually minded is life and peace.

Romans 8:6

But if the Spirit of Him who raised Jesus from the dead dwells in you, He who raised Christ from the dead will also give life to your mortal bodies through His Spirit who dwells in you.

Romans 8:11

For you did not receive the spirit of bondage again to fear, but you received the Spirit of adoption by whom we cry out, "Abba, Father." The Spirit Himself bears witness with our spirit that we are children of God, and if children, then heirs—heirs of God and joint heirs with Christ, if indeed we suffer with Him, that we also may be glorified together.

Romans 8:15-17

[God] did not spare His own Son, but delivered Him up for us all, how shall He not with Him also freely give us all things?

Romans 8:32

Who shall separate us from the love of Christ? Shall tribulation, or distress, or persecution, or famine, or nakedness, or peril, or sword? For I am persuaded that neither death nor life, nor angels nor principalities nor powers, nor things present nor things to come, nor height nor depth, nor any created thing, shall be able to separate us from the love of God which is in Christ Jesus our Lord.

Romans 8:35, 38, 39

For the message of the cross is foolishness to those who are perishing, but to us who are being saved it is the power of God.

1 Corinthians 1:18

Therefore whoever eats this bread or drinks this cup of the Lord in an unworthy manner will be guilty of the body and blood of the Lord. But let a man examine himself, and so let him eat of the bread and drink of the cup. For he who eats and drinks in an unworthy manner eats and drinks judgment to himself, not discerning the Lord's body. For this reason many are weak and sick among you, and many sleep.

1 Corinthians 11:27-30

Love [God] suffers long and is kind; love [God] does not envy; does not parade itself, is not puffed up; love [God] does not behave rudely, does not seek its own, is not provoked, thinks no evil; does not rejoice in iniquity, but rejoices in the truth; ... Love [God] never fails.

1 Corinthians 13:4-6, 8

For I delivered to you first of all that which I also received: that Christ died for our sins according to the Scriptures, and that He was buried, and that He rose again the third day according to the Scriptures, and that He was seen by Cephas, then by the twelve. After that He was seen by over five hundred brethren at once, of whom the greater part remain to the present, but some have fallen asleep. After that He was seen by James, then by all the apostles. Then last of all He was seen by me also, as by one born out of due time.

1 Corinthians 15:3-8

Now if Christ is preached that He has been raised from the dead, how do some among you say that there is no resurrection of the dead? But if there is no resurrection of the dead, then Christ is not risen. And if Christ is not risen, then our preaching is empty and your faith is also empty. Yes, and we are found false witnesses of God, because we have testified of God that He raised up Christ, whom He did not raise up—if in fact the dead do not rise. For if the dead do not rise, then Christ is not risen. And if Christ is not risen, your faith is futile; you are still in your sins!

1 Corinthians 15:12-17

Now thanks be to God who always leads us in triumph in Christ, and through us diffuses the fragrance of His knowledge in every place.

2 Corinthians 2:14

Now the Lord is the Spirit; and where the Spirit of the Lord is, there is liberty. But we all, with unveiled face, beholding as in a mirror the glory of the Lord, are being transformed into the same image from glory to glory, just as by the Spirit of the Lord.

2 Corinthians 3:17-18

For we know that if our earthly house, this tent, is destroyed, we have a building from God, a house not made with hands, eternal in the heavens. For in this we groan, earnestly desiring to be clothed with our habitation which is from heaven, if indeed, having been clothed, we shall not be found naked. For we who are in this tent groan, being burdened, not

because we want to be unclothed, but further clothed, that
mortality may be swallowed up by life.

2 Corinthians 5:1-4

Therefore, if anyone is in Christ, he is a new creation; old
things have passed away; behold, all things have become new.

2 Corinthians 5:17

Now all things are of God, who has reconciled us to Himself
through Jesus Christ, and has given us the ministry of reconciliation, that is, that God was in Christ reconciling the
world to Himself, not imputing their trespasses to them,
and has committed to us the word of reconciliation. Now
then, we are ambassadors for Christ, as though God were
pleading through us: we implore you on Christ's behalf, be
reconciled to God.

2 Corinthians 5:18-20

For He made Him who knew no sin to be sin for us, that we
might become the righteousness of God in Him.

2 Corinthians 5:21

For you know the grace of our Lord Jesus Christ, that
though He was rich, yet for your sakes He became poor,
that you through His poverty might become rich.

2 Corinthians 8:9

For though we walk in the flesh, we do not war according
to the flesh. For the weapons of our warfare are not carnal,
but mighty in God for pulling down strongholds, casting
down arguments and every high thing that exalts itself
against the knowledge of God, bringing every thought into
captivity to the obedience of Christ.

2 Corinthians 10:3-5

I have been crucified with Christ; it is no longer I who live, but Christ lives in me; and the life which I now live in the flesh I live by faith in the Son of God, who loved me and gave Himself for me.

Galatians 2:20

Christ has redeemed us from the curse of the law, having become a curse for us (for it is written, "Cursed is everyone who hangs on a tree"), that the blessing of Abraham might come upon the Gentiles in Christ Jesus, that we might receive the promise of the Spirit through faith.

Galatians 3:13-14

For you are all sons of God through faith in Christ Jesus. For as many of you as were baptized into Christ have put on Christ ... And if you are Christ's, then you are Abraham's seed, and heirs according to the promise.

Galatians 3:26-27, 29

But when the fullness of time had come, God sent forth His Son, born of a woman, born under the law, to redeem those who were under the law, that we might receive adoption as sons. And because you are sons, God has sent forth the Spirit of His Son into your hearts, crying out, "Abba, Father!" Therefore you are no longer a slave but a son, and if a son, then an heir of God through Christ.

Galatians 4:4-7

For you, brethren, have been called to liberty; only do not use liberty as an opportunity for the flesh, but through love serve one another. For all the law is fulfilled in one word, even in this: "You shall love your neighbor as yourself." But if you bite and devour one another, beware lest you be consumed by one another! I say then: Walk in the Spirit, and you shall not fulfill the lust of the flesh. For the flesh lusts against the Spirit, and the Spirit against the flesh; and these are contrary to one another, so that you do not do the things that you wish. But if you are led by the Spirit, you are not under the law.

Galatians 5:13-18

But the fruit of the Spirit is love, joy, peace, longsuffering, kindness, goodness, faithfulness, gentleness, self-control. Against such there is no law. And those who are Christ's have crucified the flesh with its passions and desires. If we live in the Spirit, let us also walk in the Spirit.

Galatians 5:22-25

But God forbid that I should boast except in the cross of our Lord Jesus Christ, by whom the world has been crucified to me, and I to the world.

Galatians 6:14

Blessed be the God and Father of our Lord Jesus Christ, who has blessed us with every spiritual blessing in the heavenly places in Christ, just as He chose us in Him before the foundation of the world, that we should be holy and without blame before Him in love, having predestined us to adoption as sons by Jesus Christ to Himself, according to the good pleasure of His will, to the praise of the glory of His grace, by which He has made us accepted in the Beloved. In Him we have redemption through His blood, the forgiveness of sins, according to the riches of His grace which He made to abound toward us in all wisdom and prudence, having made known to us the mystery of His will, according to His good pleasure which He purposed in Himself, that in the dispensation of the fullness of the times He might gather together in one all things in Christ, both which are in heaven and which are on earth—in Him. In Him also we have obtained an inheritance, being predestined according to the purpose of Him who works all things according to the counsel of His will, that we who first trusted in Christ should be to the praise of His glory. In Him also you trusted, after you heard the word of truth, the gospel of your salvation; in whom also, having believed, you were sealed with the Holy Spirit of promise.

Ephesians 1:3-13

And what is the exceeding greatness of His power toward us who believe, according to the working of His mighty power which He worked in Christ when He raised Him from the dead and seated Him at His right hand in the heavenly places, far above all principality and power and might and dominion, and every name that is named, not only in this age but also in that which is to come.

Ephesians 1:19-21

And you He made alive, who were dead in trespasses and sin...But God, who is rich in mercy, because of His great love with which He loved us, even when we were dead in trespasses, made us alive together with Christ...that in the ages to come He might show the exceeding riches of His grace in His kindness toward us in Christ Jesus. For by grace you have been saved through faith, and that not of yourselves; it is the gift of God.

Ephesians 2:1, 4, 7-8

For this reason I bow my knees to the Father of our Lord Jesus Christ, from whom the whole family in heaven and earth is named, that He would grant you, according to the riches of His glory, to be strengthened with might through His Spirit in the inner man, that Christ may dwell in your hearts through faith; that you, being rooted and grounded in love, may be able to comprehend with all the saints what is the width and length and depth and height—to know the love of Christ which passes knowledge; that you may be filled with all the fullness of God. Now to Him who is able to do exceedingly abundantly above all that we ask or think, according to the power that works in us, to Him be glory in the church by Christ Jesus to all generations, forever and ever. Amen.

Ephesians 3:14-21

Yet indeed I also count all things loss for the excellence of the knowledge of Christ Jesus my Lord, for whom I have suffered the loss of all things, and count them as rubbish, that I may gain Christ and be found in Him, not having my own righteousness, which is from the law, but that which is through faith in Christ, the righteousness which is from God by faith, that I may know Him and the power of His resurrection ...

Philippians 3:8-10

Giving thanks to the Father who has qualified us to be partakers of the inheritance of the saints in the light.

Colossians 1:12

He has delivered us from the power of darkness and conveyed us into the kingdom of the Son of His love.

Colossians 1:13

He is the image of the invisible God, the firstborn over all creation. For by Him all things were created that are in heaven and that are on earth, visible and invisible, whether thrones or dominions or principalities or powers. All things were created through Him and for Him. And He is before all things, and in Him all things consist. And He is the head of the body, the church, who is the beginning, the firstborn from the dead, that in all things He may have the preeminence.

Colossians 1:15-18

For it pleased the Father that in Him all the fullness should dwell and by Him to reconcile all things to Himself, by Him, whether things on earth or things in heaven, having made peace through the blood of His Cross. And you, who once were alienated and enemies in your mind by wicked works, yet now He has reconciled.

Colossians 1:19-21

To them God willed to make known what are the riches of the glory of this mystery among the Gentiles: which is Christ in you, the hope of glory. Him we preach, warning every man and teaching every man in all wisdom, that we may present every man perfect in Christ Jesus.

Colossians 1:27-28

For in Him dwells all the fullness of the Godhead bodily; and you are complete in Him, who is the head of all principality and power. In Him you were also circumcised with the circumcision made without hands, by putting off the body of the sins of the flesh, by the circumcision of Christ.

Colossians 2:9-11

And you, being dead in your trespasses and the uncircumcision of your flesh, He has made alive together with Him, having forgiven you all trespasses, having wiped out the handwriting of requirements that was against us, which was contrary to us. And He has taken it out of the way, having nailed it to the cross.

Colossians 2:13-14

Having disarmed principalities and powers, He made a public spectacle of them, triumphing over them in it.

Colossians 2:15

Set your mind on things above, not on things on the earth.

Colossians 3:2

For God did not appoint us to wrath, but to obtain salvation through our Lord Jesus Christ.

1 Thessalonians 5:9

But we see Jesus, who was made a little lower than the angels, for the suffering of death crowned with glory and honor, that He, by the grace of God, might taste death for everyone.

Hebrews 2:9

For it was fitting for Him, for whom are all things and by whom are all things, in bringing many sons to glory, to make the captain of their salvation perfect through sufferings. For both He who sanctifies and those who are being sanctified are all of one, for which reason He is not ashamed to call them brethren.

Hebrews 2:10-11

Inasmuch then as the children have partaken of flesh and blood, He Himself likewise shared in the same, that through death He might destroy him who had the power of death, that is, the devil, and release those who through fear of death were all their lifetime subject to bondage.

Hebrews 2:14-15

That you do not become sluggish, but imitate those who through faith and patience inherit the promises. For when God made a promise to Abraham, because He could swear by no one greater, He swore by Himself, saying, "Surely blessing I will bless you, and multiplying I will multiply you." And so, after he had patiently endured, he obtained the promise.

Hebrews 6:12-15

For men indeed swear by the greater, and an oath for confirmation is for them an end of all dispute. Thus God, determining to show more abundantly to the heirs of promise the immutability of His counsel, confirmed it by an oath, that by two immutable things, in which it is impossible for God to lie, we might have strong consolation, who have fled for refuge to lay hold of the hope set before us. This hope we have as an anchor of the soul, both sure and steadfast, and which enters the Presence behind the veil, where the forerunner has entered for us, even Jesus, having become High Priest forever according to the order of Melchizedek.

Hebrews 6:16-20

But Christ came as High Priest of the good things to come, with the greater and more perfect tabernacle not made with hands, that is, not of this creation. Not with the blood of goats and calves, but with His own blood He entered the Most Holy Place once for all, having obtained eternal redemption. For if the blood of bulls and goats and the ashes of a heifer, sprinkling the unclean, sanctifies for the purifying of the flesh, how much more shall the blood of Christ, who through the eternal Spirit offered Himself without spot to God, cleanse your conscience from dead works to serve the living God?

Hebrews 9:11-14

Without the shedding of blood there is no remission.

Hebrews 9:22

For Christ has not entered the holy places made with hands, which are copies of the true, but into heaven itself, now to appear in the presence of God for us; not that He should offer Himself often, as the high priest enters the Most Holy Place every year with blood of another—He then would have had to suffer often since the foundation of the world; but now, once at the end of the ages, He has appeared to put away sin by the sacrifice of Himself.

Hebrews 9:24-26

He who promised is faithful.

Hebrews 10:23

But without faith it is impossible to please Him, for he who comes to God must believe that He is, and that He is a rewarder of those who diligently seek Him.

Hebrews 11:6

Therefore we also, since we are surrounded by so great a cloud of witnesses, let us lay aside every weight, and the sin which so easily ensnares us, and let us run with endurance the race that is set before us, looking unto Jesus, the author and finisher of our faith, who for the joy that was set before Him endured the Cross, despising the shame, and has sat down at the right hand of the throne of God.

Hebrews 12:1-2

Therefore submit to God. Resist the devil and he will flee from you.

James 4:7

Who Himself bore our sins in His own body on the tree, that we, having died to sins, might live for righteousness— by whose stripes you were healed.

1 Peter 2:24

Be sober, be vigilant; because your adversary the devil walks about like a roaring lion, seeking whom he may devour.

1 Peter 5:8

As His divine power has given to us all things that pertain to life and godliness, through the knowledge of Him who called us by glory and virtue.

2 Peter 1:3

If we say that we have no sin, we deceive ourselves, and the truth is not in us. If we confess our sins, He is faithful and just to forgive us our sins and to cleanse us from all unrighteousness.

1 John 1:8- 9

I write to you, little children, because your sins are forgiven you for His name's sake. I write to you, fathers, because you have known Him who is from the beginning. I write to you, young men, because you have overcome the wicked one. I write to you, little children, because you have known the Father. I have written to you, fathers, because you have known Him who is from the beginning. I have written to you, young men, because you are strong, and the word of God abides in you, and you have overcome the wicked one.

1 John 2:12-14

Do not love the world or the things in the world. If anyone loves the world, the love of the Father is not in him. For all that is in the world—the lust of the flesh, the lust of the eyes, and the pride of life—is not of the Father but is of the world.

1 John 2:15-16

He who sins is of the devil, for the devil has sinned from the beginning. For this purpose the Son of God was manifested, that He might destroy the works of the devil.

1 John 3:8

God is love

1 John 4:8

In this the love of God was manifested toward us, that God has sent His only begotten Son into the world, that we might live through Him. In this is love, not that we loved God, but that He loved us and sent His Son to be the propitiation for our sins.

1 John 4:9- 10

For whatever is born of God overcomes the world. And this is the victory that has overcome the world—our faith. Who is he who overcomes the world, but he who believes that Jesus is the Son of God?

1 John 5:4-5

We know that we are of God, and the whole world lies under the sway of the wicked one.

1 John 5:19

I am He who lives, and was dead, and behold, I am alive forevermore. Amen. And I have the keys of Hades and of Death.

Revelation 1:18

And I looked, and behold, in the midst of the throne and of the four living creatures, and in the midst of the elders, stood a Lamb as though it had been slain ...

Revelation 5:6

And they sang a new song, saying: "You are worthy to take the scroll, and to open its seals; for You were slain, and have redeemed us to God by Your blood out of every tribe and tongue and people and nation, and have made us kings and priests to our God; and we shall reign on the earth."

Revelation 5:9-10

Then I heard a loud voice saying in heaven, "Now salvation, and strength, and the kingdom of our God, and the power of His Christ have come, for the accuser of our brethren, who accused them before our God day and night, has been cast down. And they overcame him by the blood of the Lamb and by the word of their testimony, and they did not love their lives to the death."

Revelation 12:10-11

ABOUT THE AUTHOR

 **Terry Moore** graduated from SMU with a degree in business administration. After graduating, Terry married his childhood sweetheart, Susan Stroube Moore, who also graduated from SMU's Class of 1973. Shortly thereafter, Terry began his career in commercial real estate and subsequently diversified into the oil & gas industry as an investor and an independent producer.

Terry and Susan became successful business owners, active in their church and community. In 1982, the couple attended a Christian Conference where they encountered the Lord in a life-changing way. The Moores then began a Bible Study in their home, which continued for four years and influenced many people who encouraged them to consider starting a church. In January 1987, Terry and Susan, along with several other couples from the Bible Study, founded Sojourn Church. This was a major shift for Terry who had never considered ministry as a career option. Under his leadership, the church continued to grow, resulting in the 1997 relocation to its current facility in Carrollton, Texas. As the membership increased with families from around the Metroplex, the Moores were instrumental in raising up leaders and planting new churches in the region.

For nearly three decades, Sojourn Church has been instrumental in coordinating and hosting conferences for thousands of participants locally and globally. Additionally, Terry and Susan partner with several local inner-city ministries, which feed the poor, offer recovery programs, provide after school programs and adult education for re-entry into mainstream society.

Terry spends much of his time preparing messages, meeting with leaders, and encouraging others. He has written a number of Bible studies designed to equip Christians to live victoriously. He serves on the board of several local ministries, as well as many international organizations.

Terry and Susan have traveled extensively around the world. They continue to be involved in a number of overseas missions where they equip pastors and church leaders with the life-changing power of Jesus Christ.

Terry is the Founding Pastor and an Elder of Sojourn Church. He and Susan have been married since 1973 and have a son and daughter in-law who have two teenage children, and daughter and son-in-law who have three young daughters.

  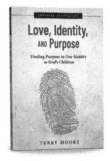

Made in USA - Kendallville, IN
36344_9781957026008
03.18.2022 1616